I0192145

# PastWord

## *Access Yesterday, the Era of Billy the Kid*

**Edited by Jan Girand**

**With Contributions by Others**

**Published by Yellow Jacket Press**
**Roswell NM**

# PastWord

## *Access Yesterday, the Era of Billy the Kid*

**Edited by Jan Girand**

**Volume 1, Issue 1, 2012**

**Owner & Producer: Jan Girand**
**Production Editor: Jan Girand**
**Copy Editor & Interior Design: Jane Nuñez Anglin**
**Genealogical & Historical Research: Charles O. Sanders**
**BTK Research & Advisor: Dr. Robert Sproull**
**Layout & Preparation for Publication: Kathy Cook**
**Cover & Logo Design: Kathy Avery**

**Copyright 2012 by Jan Girand, all rights reserved. Without written permission by the author, editor & publisher, no part of this book may be reproduced by any mechanical, photographic or electronic means, or in the form of an audio recording, nor may be stored in a retrieval system, transmitted or otherwise copied for public or private use other than "fair use."**

**Yellow Jacket Press**
**P.O. Box 386**
**Roswell NM 88202**

Library of Congress Cataloging-in-Publication Data
Girand, Jan
PastWord, Access Yesterday, the Era of Billy the Kid, by Jan Girand
ISBN 978-0-615-66111-7

# Dedication Page

*PastWord© is dedicated to my mother, Verna Laumbach Sparks (1909—1996) who taught me the value of family history, mine as well as others, and a fascination for and appreciation of the rich history of our New Mexico.*

*She first wrote* **Piñons** *when she attended college at New Mexico Normal, Las Vegas, New Mexico, in the very early 1930s. When she wrote it, she had Santa Fe in mind, where lived her aunt and uncle, Estefanita Laumbach and Jesus Sito Candelario. She was also thinking of her father's childhood home at Buena Vista in northern New Mexico, and her own childhood home that they called Cedar Springs Ranch in the rugged Canadian River Gorge and LaCinta Canyon country.*

## Piñons
### By Verna Laumbach

Out of the emptiness of evening air
from streets where dead leaves sighed of coming frost,
I came into rooms sweet with piñons, where
old memories rushed back, once nearly lost.

I saw again a dim cathedral filled
with incense of piñons, where tired souls
found rest. And quaint adobe homes where skilled
brown hands turned piñons over open coals,
and children looked on, with names
long forgotten, but eager as the flames.

I traveled back to woods that once I knew
at home, where piñons fell, ungathered, free,
on carpets of soft needles where winds blew
and stirred a fragrance old as memory.

*Oil Painting by Verna L. Sparks*

# Table of Contents

*PastWord*© gives readers access to the past, back to the era—spanning the eighteen-hundreds—and the area—a large part of New Mexico—of Billy the Kid Bonney and Pat Garrett, their associates and contemporaries. Its annual issues will not be limited to just Billy and Pat, however.  As researcher Charles O. "Butch" Sanders said, too much has been written and said about Billy, pushing into obscurity other characters more worthy of mention. The issues of *PastWord*© will more than just mention many worthy historical characters of that era and area in New Mexico.

But first, let's:

## FOLLOW THE TRAIL OF BILLY BONNEY AND PAT GARRETT
### By Jan Girand

Amble through the heart of New Mexico, experience the legend, follow the trail of Billy the Kid Bonney, Patrick Garrett and their contemporaries.

The Territory of New Mexico, in the 1870s and 1880s, had a wave of rampant lawlessness, unparalleled in the history of the U.S. However, one must walk a mile in their boots and moccasins before making conclusions about the wild ways of the men and boys, and also women, of that era. To be fair to our ancestors and those who lived among them, we must consider the times in which they lived, and the way of life conditions thrust upon them.

Many historians believe Henry McCarty, alias William H. "Kid" Antrim, alias William H. Bonney, alias Billy the Kid, was born in the east, most say in a desperately poor borough tenement of New York City to an Irish lass or lassie—married or unmarried. That is only conjecture. Once tentatively stated in print, then repeated hundreds of times thereafter by other writers, makes people think it is fact. However, it is unproven. No one really knows Billy's origins. Only a little is known about him and his family prior to his arrival in New Mexico. It is known that he came to New Mexico in the 1870s and, after the death of his mother, Catherine Antrim, he started out on his own, still a kid, from Silver City.

As an unknown kid, Billy bounced around from Arizona to Mexico and back to the New Mexico Territory. He became involved in the infamous Lincoln County War after the cold-blooded shooting of his befriender, Englishman John Henry Tunstall. That was a time in New Mexico of bitter political strife and financial power struggles. Many times situations occurred where it was either kill or be killed. They had to do what they had to do to survive.

Billy vowed vengeance on all who participated in the cruel, wanton murder of his friend, John Tunstall. Later, he was involved in the deaths of Morton, Baker, McCloskey, Brady, Hindman, and Beckwith. That vendetta led him through the heart of New Mexico. It took him to Blazer's Mill, near Mescalero, where Brewer and Buckshot Roberts met their deaths. The Rio Ruidoso led him to Dowlin's Mill, and the Hondo Valley led to John Chisum's South Springs Ranch near Roswell. The Pecos River trail went to old Fort Sumner, where Joe Grant caused his own demise. A dim trail led east to Los Portales Springs hideout. At Seven Rivers Crossing, near Carlsbad, 200,000 head of cattle from Texas were tallied following the Goodnight-Loving-Chisum Trails. Were Billy and his pals drawn there too, with rustling intent?

Patrick Floyd Garrett, born in Alabama to a wealthy plantation-owning family, had been a successful buffalo hunter in Texas before drifting into New Mexico. His election as sheriff of Lincoln County drew him into Billy's legend. In 1800, Lincoln County was comprised of 27,000 square miles, the largest county in the U.S. It was nearly a quarter of New Mexico, bigger than Connecticut, Delaware, Massachusetts, Rhode Island, and Vermont put together.

Most historians know Patrick Garrett as having been a good sheriff when New Mexico needed such a man. Many historians also say Billy Bonney and Pat Garrett had once been friends.

Posse member Jim Carlisle died, following the White Oaks skirmish on December 1, 1880 in a shooting at the Greathouse Stage Station near Corona. Billy's trail goes on to Anton Chico, Puerto de Luna, Sunnyside Spring and Old Fort Sumner, where Tom Folliard fell mortally wounded in an ambush. (Note: Tom's surname was not O'Folliard. He might have had middle initial O. His name has been miswritten many times, including on his fairly modern grave marker.) Connections to the Wilcox-Yerby ranches and Brazil Spring played a part in Billy's surrender at Stinking Springs, east of Fort Sumner, where the life of Billy's pal, Charlie Bowdre, ended. On Billy went, now as a prisoner, to Las Vegas (New Mexico) by wagon, and after a restless mob tried to take Billy, to Santa Fe by railcar. He spent three months in Santa Fe's jail waiting for April and the beginning of the spring session of the District Court at Mesilla. From Santa Fe, he was eventually taken to old Mesilla for trial. There, after a guilty verdict and the judge's sentence for Billy to be hanged in Lincoln, he was taken under armed guard by wagon through La Luz and what would become Alamogordo, back to Lincoln. However, at Lincoln, he performed his famed daring escape after killing Bell and Olinger. (That escape has been reenacted in Old Town Lincoln late every summer for decades.)

After leaving Lincoln, instead of going to Mexico as he should have, with the help of friends, Billy got rid of his shackles, went to Las Tablas, and after crossing the Capitan Gap, eventually made it back to Fort Sumner. There, he had friends and, legends say, at least one sweetheart. Whether that sweetheart was Paulita Maxwell remains unproven; she herself said not. But Paulita was, at least, his friend. Some say Billy's pal, Pedro Maxwell, had betrayed the Kid's whereabouts to Sheriff Garrett, setting him up to be killed, because his sister Paulita was sweet on him. One thing is certain: Her son, Telesfor, could not have been Billy's, as was sometimes written. And surely Celsa was not his girlfriend, as some writers claimed; she was a married woman with children, and sister of Sheriff Pat Garrett's wife.

Much of what has been written about Billy has been speculation, at best, and more often, pure fiction.

Were Garrett and his posse really hot on Billy's trail? Or was it pure luck that they stumbled upon him in Fort Sumner? It was there—at what had once been a federal military fort at Bosque Redondo— in Pedro Maxwell's sweltering bedroom the night of July 14, 1881, that Pat Garrett killed the Kid by taking him by surprise. Pat was also surprised.

Billy's national fame had begun with his breakout at Lincoln. After his death, he became immortalized worldwide in books, movies, legends and songs. Young Billy was buried near his pals in the old Fort Sumner cemetery. In 1981, because his modern-day headstone was repeatedly vandalized, and his footstone twice stolen, a permanent wrought-iron cage was set around marked graves covered with cement. Now Billy spends eternity behind bars—if in fact he does lie within that barred space. Charlie Foor and the Dudrow Map make it seem likely that he instead lies a few yards away.

Charlie Foor, born in Kentucky in 1850, came to Fort Sumner in 1881 and died there in 1940. Records show that Foor arrived within three-and-a-half months after Billy's demise, which adds credence to Foor's almost first-hand knowledge of the exact location of Billy's grave. Foor was a contemporary and friend of many in Fort Sumner who knew Billy well. He and the Charles W. Dudrow Map indicate Billy was not buried exactly where his modern marker proclaims. This spatial nit-picking only matters when someone wants to disinter his, and his mother's, remains for DNA testing.

Go where you will, over the many trails he rode, and you will find that Billy the Kid Bonney still rides, and still lives loose in New Mexico.

Patrick Garrett's trail, after Billy's death, took him many places, including Texas. His trail led to mines in the Jicarilla Mountains, and he made numerous land deals. He was also a gambler and often lost assets. He was drawn to the Roswell area, where he, and later his daughter, Elizabeth, made their homes for some years. New Mexico history researcher Mike Pitel believes Garrett was happiest when living in Roswell. Garrett's two-story family home was a few miles east of Roswell, now on private property. There will be more about this property later in this issue. Elizabeth's home was a small adobe in Roswell on South Lea. Both structures survive them. Near Roswell, Garrett had begun to establish an irrigation canal—a grandiose plan, where he sunk a large investment of effort and money, which he could ill afford to lose, and ultimately did. Wealthy railroad contractor, J.J. Hagerman, invested in this canal; it was later named for him and he was credited for building it. This canal still provides irrigation to Pecos Valley farmers.

*Patrick Garrett, photo taken by J. Furlong, Las Vegas, NM; Richard Weddle collection*

Before Garrett had altogether left law enforcement, as Sheriff of Dona Ana County, he followed the trail of Albert Fountain and his young son, Henry, trying to solve their apparent murder near White Sands, which remains an enduring New Mexico mystery. That investigation earned him more enemies.

On February 29, 1908, he was traveling by wagon with Carl Adamson and Wayne Brazel near the Organ Mountains to discuss the sale of his property. Brazel, a sheep or goat rancher, was leasing Garrett's ranch in Dona Ana County. When Pat stopped and got out of the wagon, turning his back on those present for privacy while urinating, unarmed and trusting, he was shot in the back of his head, and shot again where he fell. Wayne Brazel rode into Mesilla to announce he had shot Garrett. Later in court, he claimed self-defense. The Mesilla jury acquitted Brazel of any wrong-doing. Many individuals, some politically well known, were suspected of plotting that ambush of Garrett, of even pulling the trigger, but were not tried. There was never another trial concerning the former lawman's cold-blooded murder.

Garrett' final resting place is in the Masonic cemetery in Las Cruces. It was Leon Metz, historian-author, who had appropriately pointed out at the end of his biographical book—*Pat Garrett, The Story of a Western Lawman*—that, except for his grave marker, New Mexico had no monument to the man who had played such an important role to this state's history.

This omission was finally rectified in March 2012 with the dedication of Patrick Garrett's majestic bronze statue by renowned Texan sculptor Robert Summers.

Both Bonney and Garrett left indelible marks in New Mexico's history. Some of what made them lasting are these enduring, unanswered mysteries: From where did Billy and his family come? What was his origin? Why cannot historians find genealogy, census and other permanent records of his early life? From where did he get his assumed name, Bonney? What actually happened to Albert and young Henry Fountain, and why? Their cold case was only indirectly connected to Billy, but directly connected to Pat

Garrett, who was assigned to solve it. Who really killed Pat Garrett? And why? Were several people involved in the conspiracy and planning of that murder? Who were they?

While living in Roswell, Patrick Garrett's blind daughter, Elizabeth, wrote New Mexico's state song, *O Fair New Mexico*, adopted a few years after New Mexico became the 47th U.S. state.

The enduring legends of Billy Bonney, Patrick Garrett and their contemporaries are tightly woven into the colorful fabric of the history of New Mexico, which received statehood status only one hundred years ago this year, on January 6, 1912. Some claim that delay was because the country of the United States—then established for 136 years—had until then deemed the Territory of New Mexico as too wild and lawless for statehood. It took more than sixty years of trying before it was accepted as a state. Throughout 2012, New Mexico—all parts of it—is holding centennial events to celebrate its statehood.

*Lincoln County Courthouse as it appears today, now a museum. It was originally the Murphy Dolan store and after it was sold, became the courthouse with an upstairs room used as a jail. In 1881 the building looked slightly different. There were no outside stairs going to the upper balcony. Billy, held prisoner upstairs, stood in the upper left-hand window when he shot Olinger coming across the road from the Wortley with prisoners.*

**In 1880, Lincoln County, at more than 27,000 square miles, was the largest county in the United States. It was nearly a quarter of New Mexico, bigger than Connecticut, Delaware, Massachusetts, Rhode Island and Vermont put together.**

## New Mexico's Centennial
### By Jan Girand

New Mexico officially celebrated its 100th year of statehood on January 6, 2012, but continues to celebrate all year with multiple events throughout the state that are geared toward this once in a lifetime anniversary.

Our state may be one of the youngest of the United States of America, but it is not a young place, as places in the United States go. New Mexico has still-existing sites that go back more than a thousand years. Archaeologists and anthropologists believe evidence found in eastern New Mexico shows Clovis Man and his kin were the first people to populate the Americas at least 13,000 years ago. And the Folsom Point, found in northeastern New Mexico, dates man in the Americas a mere one or two thousand years more recently than old man Clovis. The 1,000 year old Taos Pueblo is known as the oldest continually inhabited community in the United States. The Indian pueblo of Acoma was founded in 1300. Hispanic Europeans founded our state capitol, Santa Fe, the City of Holy Faith, in 1610, before Pilgrims landed at Plymouth.

As far as we now know, early New Mexico societies began with the Anasazis, whom the state's Indians call "the Ancient Ones" or "Those Who Came Before," believe to be the ancestors or close kin of the inhabitants of the now existing nineteen pueblos in western and northern New Mexico. Ruins of settlements of the Anasazi near Santa Fe have been dated at 1150 to 1350 AD. European explorers from Spain came in the 1500s to colonize the area for their king and god. Generations later, Anglo "Americans" discovered this place and made it their home. Over the centuries, New Mexico became known as a land of three cultures: Indians, Hispanics and Anglos. Signifying its "modern" history, this land has had several flags fly above its capitol in Santa Fe: Spain, Mexico, Confederate —briefly, and Union. Since 1846, the American flag has endured. Under Spanish rule for centuries, this was an inhospitable place for outsiders, but under the Mexican flag, it welcomed foreign trade, that is, trade "from the States." With the advent of the Santa Fe Trail, commerce in New Mexico became profitable and introduced the area to the world, and the world to New Mexico.

New Mexico has a long history, but has also played important modern roles with its Los Alamos National Laboratory that—with development of the first atomic bomb detonated at White Sands' Trinity Site in 1945—brought the dreadful Second World War to an end, and led to many peaceful innovations.

Yet to many far beyond its borders, New Mexico is still most noted for its Wild West history. We look to our future by looking at our past.

# Journey to Cimarron over the Historic Santa Fe Trail of Northeastern New Mexico
by Jan Girand

*This article was first published in the Byways section of the 14th issue of the Roswell Web Magazine (www.roswellwbmagazine.com), where it is still archived.*

The Santa Fe Trail began in Franklin, Missouri and ended in Santa Fe, New Mexico. Although Indians had been using this route for centuries, William Becknell and his wagons officially established the Trail in late 1821. Before and thereafter, it was used for their varied purposes by mountain men and trappers, explorers, topographical engineers, early settlers, traders of commerce vital to the new frontier, seekers of gold and other treasures, military expeditions and their journalists who accompanied them.

The most important of the latter group was, in 1846, the Army of the West, led into New Mexico by Brigadier General Stephen Watts Kearney, and Colonel of the First Regiment Missouri Volunteers, Alexander W. Doniphan. The journalists accompanying them recorded their not-so-easy journey, and their amazingly easy take-over, "without firing a shot," of New Mexico from Mexico, making it the then-newest acquisition and territory of the United States.

Early Santa Fe Trail wagon travelers from Missouri and Kansas, wanting to avoid the hazardous high mountain Raton Pass between Colorado and New Mexico, took the Cimarron Cut-Off that cut across the corner of the Oklahoma panhandle, entering New Mexico's northeastern corner just above what is now Clayton and the Kiowa National Grasslands. From there, that branch of the Trail headed southwesterly, passing beside the Point of Rocks (near the now historic Dorsey Mansion at Chico Spring), where Indians ambushed a wagon-train, massacring the James White family, including wife Ann and young daughter Virginia, in October 1849.

That branch continued past what is now Springer, crossing the Canadian River. From there onward to Santa Fe, I-25 now runs beside that branch of the old Santa Fe Trail. Deep wagon ruts can still be seen in places, attesting to the fact that for 150 years, settlers have not plowed their prairies for planting, but let their cattle roam, grazing the grass of the undisturbed land.

Why they called this route the Cimarron Cut-Off is hard to figure since this branch did not pass by Cimarron. From Springer, it went south to Wagon Mound, passing beside two volcanic formations, one of which resembles a covered wagon drawn by a team of horses, its sharply defined shape against the blue sky visible for miles, rising up from the floor of the high prairie. That branch went on southward, close beside I-25 that now follows it, to what is now Watrous, but was then called La Junta because there two rivers joined. Just above La Junta, at Valmora, two branches of the Santa Fe Trail—this Cimarron Cut-Off and the Mountain Route—converged, becoming one again as it continued on to Santa Fe at the Trail's end.

The Trail's rugged Mountain Route—"the Santa Fe Trail via Bent's Fort, 1822-1879"—came in from Colorado, crossed the high Raton Pass, entering New Mexico above what is now the town of Raton. At about where the NRA Whittington Center is located, in front of some of Colfax County's coal-rich mesas, that route branched into two for a few miles. At that point, below a bare rock jutting above the mesa, those two smaller branches ran roughly parallel to each other, separated by just a few miles. Both crossed the Vermejo and Cimarron rivers. The more westerly one passed through what is now the village of Cimarron in front of the mountains to its west, and both converged, becoming one again, near picturesque Rayado, now owned by the Boy Scouts of America.

In the saddle of the mountains at Rayado, not far from the foot of the Tooth of Time rock formation, Lucien Maxwell built his first home, later given to his kinsman, Jesus Abreu (pronounced Hey SUS Ah BRA uh). Jesus Abreu's wife, Petra Beaubien (pronounced PA trah Bo BE uhn), built the nearby Rayado Chapel around 1902. That chapel and the Abreu home, now belonging to the Boy Scouts of America, are some of Rayado's historical landmarks.)

*The Abreu house at Rayado, photo by Jan Girand*

From Rayado, the Santa Fe Trail's Mountain Route went south, passing through the high green picturesque valley at Ocate, crossing the Ocate Creek, then continued directly south, passing the sites where Fort Union would soon be built. Then onward it went to the fertile grasslands of Valmora and LaJunta (pronounced Lah HOON tah), where it joined the Cimarron Cut-Off into the singular Santa Fe Trail that continued south to Las Vegas, then for a few miles in a westerly direction, to the Trail's end destination, Santa Fe.

Until the construction of the Santa Fe Railroad, completed in northeastern New Mexico in 1879 and 1880, the Santa Fe Trail was a vital commercial trailway, linking the established east to the fledgling west.

A fur trapper from Illinois, Lucien Boneparte Maxwell came to northeastern New Mexico, met French-Canadian Charles Beaubien, who had established his Mexican citizenship (New Mexico was then under Mexican rule) after marrying an Hispanic woman from a prominent New Mexico family. By 1840, Beaubien had become a wealthy property-owner in Taos. Maxwell married his friend's lovely eldest daughter, Luz. They had nine children.

An interesting note: Peter Maxwell was the eldest son of Lucien and Luz Beaubien Maxwell. On July 14, 1881, Sheriff Pat Garrett gunned down Billy "the Kid" Bonney in Pete's dark bedroom at Lucien B. Maxwell's final home at Fort Sumner, which had not long before been a federal military installation and enforced reservation for Navajo and Jicarilla Apache Indians.

Some historians say Billy and Paulita had only been friends. Others say Pete's next-to-the-youngest sister, Paulita, was Billy's favorite sweetheart, and the reason he returned to Fort Sumner after he escaped from his hanging engagement at Lincoln. A part of that version says that was why Pete Maxwell betrayed Billy's whereabouts to Garrett. That betrayal was one of several unproven speculations about why Garrett could successfully surprise and kill the Kid.

Deluvina Maxwell—an Indian girl adopted by the Maxwells when she was a child—was another who loved Billy like a brother, and was present at Fort Sumner to mourn the death of the Kid the next day.

After Lucien Maxwell had sold the huge Grant for $1,350,000 to a group of English investors in 1870, he and his family moved to Fort Sumner. He purchased the fort and everything on the land, but could not buy the land it sat upon; the U.S. Government maintained that ownership.

The new owners of the vast grant began trying to get rid of the many settlers and Indians on the land. That resulted in the 1875 Colfax County War. Ownership of the grant land changed hands several times, next to a Dutch investment group.

Presently, most of what had been Maxwell Grant land is owned by four private ranches: the vast Vermijo Park (WS) Ranch, now owned by media mogul Ted Turner; the UU Bar Ranch that has been, off and on, embroiled in disputes with hunters wanting access to federal lands; the Charles Springer (CS) Ranch, long-time owned by respected ranchers Les and Linda Mitchell Davis; and the Philmont Scout Ranch. The National Forest Service also manages a large portion of the original Maxwell Land Grant.

The village of Cimarron—at an elevation of 6,542 feet, situated on the eastern slope of the Sangre de Cristo Mountains, yet also alongside the great plains of northeastern New Mexico—is known for many things.

In the early and mid-1800s, it was known as a lawless place where famous bad guys hid out or flaunted their desperado ways, and where lawmen and others of famed repute also gathered. In addition to Lucien B. Maxwell, some of its famous residents or visitors included Christopher "Kit" Carson, Buffalo Bill Cody, Annie Oakley, Wyatt Earp, bad-boys Frank and Jesse James, Clay Allison and bank robber Black Jack Ketchum—who ultimately lost his head at Clayton. It is said that Billy the Kid Bonney, of southeastern New Mexico, also visited.

Cimarron was known as the seat of the vast 1,714,765-acre Maxwell Land Grant because that was where its singular grantee, Lucien B. Maxwell, built his second home, ten years after establishing his first headquarters beside the Rayado River. He had later given that Rayado land and home to his wife's brother, Jesus Abreu (born 1823, died 1900), and moved his operations to where he built his newer home in 1858 on the banks of the Cimarron River, at what is now the village of Cimarron, then named "Maxwell's Ranché." His was a place known for its open hospitality to anyone who stopped by, including countless Indians.

In the communal campground in a central plaza of Cimarron, at the point where the Santa Fe Trail entered the town, a well was dug in 1871. It benefited the freighters and their beasts of burden as they passed through, hauling goods from Kansas Territory to Fort Union. The now-existing gazebo was reconstructed in 1962 based upon early photographs.

Henri Lambert—once cook for General U.S. Grant and President Abraham Lincoln—built the St. James Hotel in 1880. At least twenty-six murders were committed in that historic building during the Territory's lawless days. Henri's son, Fred Lambert, at age 23, became the youngest member of New Mexico's Territorial Mounted Police, which became the New Mexico Mounted Police in January 1912, when New Mexico was admitted to the union. At that time, that state police force, mounted on horseback, had only six officers to protect the entire state. The New Mexico Mounted Police was the forerunner of the New Mexico State Police. In more modern times, Fred Lambert was a memorable Cimarron figure and instrumental in preserving the old Aztec Grist Mill and turning it into a museum. [*I knew Fred Lambert in his latter years.*]

The Mill was originally built to provide wheat flour and cornmeal for local residents and soldiers. When the Indian agency at Taos was relocated to Cimarron in 1861, from the Mill blankets, food and other staples were dispensed to the Indians. In 1875, there was a minor Indian uprising at the Mill. In 1876, the Indian Agency at Cimarron was closed and the Indians were moved to a reservation in northwestern New Mexico and Colorado.

Lucien and Luz Maxwell built the Immaculate Conception Church in Cimarron in 1864 after the death of their child, Verenisa, in her memory. Jean Baptiste Lamy, Santa Fe's first bishop, dedicated it, which had begun as a mission church. It was enlarged in 1909 and the new bell and bell-tower were dedicated the next year.

Two graves—that of Verenisa Maxwell (1860-1864) and the child's maternal grandmother, Maria Pabla Beaubien (1811-1864)—were placed behind Maxwell's family home at Cimarron. The large two-story Maxwell Ranché building partially burned in 1888, and the rest was destroyed by fire in 1924. The original Maxwell home is gone but those two gravesites remain. Pabla was the wife of one of the two original land grantees, Charles Beaubien (1800-1864).

Stockyards, warehouses and supply stores were vital for the safekeeping and selling of goods and wares hauled or driven over the Trail. M.R. Whiteman first built a still existing building in Cimarron as a freighting depot for the Andres Daws stage-line. The Dold Brothers, who ran a freight-line between Missouri and Las Vegas, New Mexico, later used it as a warehouse; it is still known as the Dold Brothers' Warehouse. It was a trading post and Indian Agency in 1861, and also Lucien Maxwell's commissary. Twelve years later, Asa F. Middaugh and Henry Miller Porter briefly used it as a general store. For a while, it was also the home of the Cimarron News and Press. Since 1908, it has been the private home of the Lail family.

Cimarron is now somewhat off the beaten path, but it was once on a path well-traveled, and an important town on the western frontier.

In summer after rains, its setting is green and crisp as the mountain air surrounding it. Historical Cimarron is a great place to visit or stay a while. The St. James has its welcome mat out, a place set and a bed made. They even have a lamp or two burning for you.

=-=-=-=-=-=-=-=-=-=-=-=-=-=-=-=-=-=-=-=-=-=-=-=-=-=-=-=-=-=-=-=-=-=-=-=

# West of the Pecos
By Jan Girand

*Rio Pecos near Villanueva, photo by Jan Girand*

In the latter 1700s and the 1800s, "West of the Pecos" was synonymous with the Wild West—the still unsettled and uncivilized frontier of the United States.

Aldolph Bandelier said the name Pecos was first written by Juan de Oñate in his reports about an Indian pueblo.

The Pecos River begins north of Pecos, New Mexico at an elevation of 12,000 feet in the Santa Fe Mountain range in Mora County. Soon after leaving its headwaters in Mora, it meanders southeast in New Mexico, parallel to but considerably east of the Rio Grande, until it enters the southern portion of West Texas and flows, still southeasterly, to ultimately empty into the Rio Grande near Del Rio, Texas.

Man eventually built multiple dams on the Pecos to domestically utilize its waters. That, and the arid west's dire need for water, caused long-lasting strife and lawsuits between New Mexico and Texas, until the federal government intervened to settle it with the 1949 Pecos River Compact. But still, friction concerning desperately needed water between the two states continued until their 2003 legal settlement.

Those dams drastically changed the appearance of the Pecos after Europeans first saw it. Then, it was said that its water was fast-moving, and the river was from sixty-five to one hundred feet wide, and seven to ten feet deep, with few safe crossings for man or beast.

The river valley was settled by the Pecos Pueblo Indians around 800 A.D. Francisco Vazquez de Coronado and his conquistadors were the first recorded Europeans to see and cross it, around 1541. In 1583, Spaniard Antonio de Espejo called it Rio de Las Vacas because he and his band saw many buffalo in the region.

San Miguel del Bado in the upper valley of the Pecos was one of the nation's earliest European settlements, founded around 1636. A short while after Espejo spied the river, Gaspar Castaño de Sosa came along and called it the Rio Salado because of its undrinkable salty water. For the same reason, Mexicans, when the territory was theirs, called it the Rio Puerco, dirty river, or river of pigs.

When Anglo Americans began to come into New Mexico with their cattle drives, their primary route was along the Pecos. Several large cattle ranches were established in the Pecos River valley of New Mexico and Texas.

=-=-=-=-=-=-=-=-=-=-=-=-=-=-=-=-=-=-=-=-=-=-=-=-=-=-=-=-=-=-=-=-=-=-=-=-=-=-=-=

## NORA TRUE JOHNSON HENN

### Historian and Chronicler of the Lincoln County War

### By Frederick Nolan

*Originally a group photo with Nora Henn by Bob McCubbin, courtesy of Frederick Nolan;*
*photo enhancement by Charles O. Sanders*

The town of Lincoln New Mexico, up in the mountains between Roswell and Albuquerque, is one of the great treasures of the American West. Right here, in the very same buildings where Billy the Kid fought for his life, you are closer to history than practically anywhere in the United States. It's a small place, with several museums in buildings unchanged since the 1870s when the entire region was consumed by the so-called Lincoln County War, in which it was said something like 200 men died. So powerful has the legend of Billy the Kid become, that for many decades he and he alone has attracted more visitors to New Mexico than anything else the state has to offer.

Sometimes it seems as if everyone who comes to Lincoln wants only to know whether it's true that Billy the Kid killed 21 men – one for every year of his life – but the ever-patient State Monument staff and the volunteers from the Lincoln County Historical Society listen patiently, and do their best to answer the question (no he didn't) and the many other queries visitors have. As well as the tourists however, there is also a steady and regular flow of historians, newspapermen, and television feature makers, all in the process of writing books, articles, or films about those gaudy frontier days. And always, always, they ended up talking to a sweet little old lady who lived in a charmingly idiosyncratic, book-packed adobe house west of town. Her name was Nora Henn.

Nora True Johnson Henn was born on May 23, 1925, the daughter of Albert Johnson and Nora Murray Johnson of Dallas, Texas. After high school, Nora moved to Los Angeles to care for relatives and it was there she met and married Walter Henn on June 27, 1945. They lived for a while in Rochester, New York, where they worked for Kodak and also operated a newsstand and soda shop. In the early 60s they moved to Texas, and from there, in 1965, she and Walter, a very talented painter, moved to Lincoln. This was at a time when– apart from the annual Billy the Kid Pageant, in which most of the residents of Lincoln played the parts of the Kid and Pat Garrett and all the other characters involved in the Lincoln County War –facilities for tourists were, to put it mildly, pretty basic. The town itself was rundown such an extent that there was nowhere visitors could even buy a cup of coffee, but within a few years Nora and Walter started waking people up to the treasure under their feet and all around them. They were instrumental in organizing the Lincoln County Historical Society, as well as the historical ordinance which keeps Lincoln looking pretty much the way it looked in Billy the Kid's time, something tourists today delight in. Walter was the first director of the Lincoln County Heritage Trust, and he and Nora were largely responsible for the restoration of a number of the town's historical buildings.

Over those years their home, Casa Gallinas (they couldn't resist the joke), became a sort of informal historical enquiry desk for anyone passing through town who was interested in real history as opposed to the comic book kind. By the middle 70s it had become one of the least-secret secret gardens in the entire state, and every writer, every researcher, every TV filmmaker who came down the pike made it a point to drop in and get up to speed. Throughout all this time, while Walter devoted himself to the rehabilitation of Lincoln and recording its historical buildings in painting after painting after painting, Nora buried herself in the minutiae of the Lincoln County War to such an extent that one historian said she not only knew the history, she even knew the gossip of the period.

Day-by-day, inch-by-inch, everything recorded in her impeccable handwriting, she ferreted out from descendants and old-timers the stories of all the families that peopled the area, stories that would otherwise have been lost forever. In the process she became the mentor and friend of many of the writers – and I do mean many – who came to Lincoln to study its history, myself among them. I think it would be fair to say that there is not a single book about Billy the Kid and or the Lincoln County War that was written between 1970 and the present day which did not benefit in some way from Nora's input.

After Walter died in 1999, she continued to work on the several projects she kept going rather in the way that a juggler keeps balls in the air – a history of the Lincoln County War, a complete history of the state of New Mexico from its Spanish beginnings to the present day, and a study of the Machiavellian group of politicians, lawyers, businessmen, and crooks who controlled New Mexico politics (and most of its money) during its Territorial days. Right to the very end she resisted every appeal from her many friends to get them into print – something to do with not wishing to ever have to read her own reviews.

She is survived by a niece, Rebecca Leger, of Canada, and her family. Although Nora never had any biological offspring, it can truly be said she did, in fact, have many children – those mentioned above as well as many others. It was said of her that she had probably forgotten more of Lincoln's history than anyone will ever know, and it was true. Of all of the many, many historians who have applied their talents to telling the story of the life and times of Billy the Kid, none has ever been more cherished than Nora Henn, and none has ever been such good company.

*Nora True Johnson Henn, born Dallas, Texas, May 23, 1925; married Walter Henn, June 27, 1945, died Lincoln, New Mexico, May 13, 2011*

Editor's Note: Frederick Nolan, author, publishing company editor and executive, was born in Liverpool, England in 1931, and educated in Liverpool and Aberaeron, Wales. He began writing about the American southwest at age twenty-one. He has written many fictional novels under various pen names, but he is best known in our region as the author of non-fiction books, including: *The Life and Death of John Henry Tunstall; The Lincoln County War, a Documentary History; The West of Billy the Kid*; the *Wild West: History Myth and the Making of America*; and *Tascosa, Its Life and Gaudy Times*.

## Frederick Nolan and Pals
### By Jan Girand

PastWord Editor Jan Girand took this photo of Frederick Nolan on a rainy Monday, September 27, 2004, in the midst of the Battle for Billy's Bones. The occasion was an eclectic gathering for a scheduled hearing in Fort Sumner, New Mexico. Three men—Tom Sullivan, Steve Sederwall and Gary Graves—had filed a petition in the 10th District Court to exhume the remains of Billy, and filed a petition in the 6th Judicial Court to exhume his mama, Catherine, in Silver City for DNA comparison. But the communities of Fort Sumner and Silver City, and other individuals, opposed them.

During pre-hearing negotiations the previous Friday, "at the 11th hour," the three men dropped their cases, with prejudice (a legal term meaning they could reopen the cases). However, many interested folks had already gathered, or were on their way to Fort Sumner, so an unstructured gathering prevailed on Monday, September 27, 2004. Nolan, from England, seen here with his fresh red, white and blue bouquet, which he laid on the marked Pals graves, was one of those gathered that day.

Billy's life was full of unanswered mysteries; here was a modern mystery: Who, in the stealth of that night, broke into the padlocked "cage" surrounding the graves and destroyed this bouquet and did no other vandalism?

Background information for the occasion of this gathering: In 2003, Lincoln County Sheriff Tom Sullivan; Capitan mayor and deputized deputy, Steve Sederwall; and De Baca County Sheriff Gary Graves publically began planning to exhume the remains of Billy Bonney in Fort Sumner and his mother's, Catherine Antrim, in Silver City for DNA comparison to establish that Billy really was buried at Fort Sumner. The communities and mayors of both Fort Sumner and Silver City blocked their attempts.

History shows that the Fort Sumner Cemetery had been washed out by the Pecos River of 1904, and some remains, many unidentified, were exposed and had to be reburied.

Billy's original grave marker had been gone for many years. A headstone was placed for the Kid in 1932 even though those placing it did not know exact location of his remains.

It was likely that Catherine Antrim was originally placed in an unmarked grave in the Silver City cemetery. That cemetery was sold in 1882, and the site purchaser was required to relocate the graves outside the city. Did he properly move stones and markers with their pertinent bodies? When they were moved, were multiple remains placed in the same grave?

A modern headstone was placed in Catherine's memory but there is no way to know exactly where her actual remains are located.

# JOURNEY THROUGH OLD LINCOLN TOWN AND FORT STANTON

## By Jan Girand

Reprinted from the Archives of the RoswellWebMagazine in BYWAYS Issue 04, published more than a decade ago:

In [an earlier rwm] issue, we took a daytrip, beginning from Roswell, through the Hondo Valley and turned left at the fork, ending up in Ruidoso before returning home. *Go to http://roswellwebmagazine.com, click on Archives, Issue 2, if you want to review it.*

On this issue's daytrip, we turn right at the highway fork and head to Lincoln and Ft. Stanton.

The weather is comfortably warm; it is a great day for adventure. Grab your camera; I've got mine.

This is a good photo opportunity day because the sky is almost back to its clear blue and the wind is calm. Just days earlier, neither was the case. For much of a week, the sky—even in Roswell—was hazy with smoke because strong winds added to the dangerously dry timber conditions spreading a fire in the mountainous Mayhill area, destroying at least twenty structures there, including homes. Only a day or two before our trip, the fire was finally under control and out.

We leave town heading west on Highway 70-380. As the new four-lane highway continues to progress westward, we pass highway construction. Ahead we vaguely see the small teepee-shaped Capitan Mountain, the northern tip of it, its pale blue blending into sky the nearly same blue hue. We see the mountain better on most days when the sky is clear without lingering smoke. Today, we will soon see the Capitan much closer and from a different perspective; it will then not at all resemble a teepee.

The picturesque Hondo Valley is rich in history; it has seen both placid and turbulent times. Its most turbulent days were during the Lincoln County Wars, when the residents' loyalties were sharply divided between two factions. Even now, 125 years later, the loyalties of some residents of Lincoln and Chaves Counties are still divided. Those include descendents of those who played lead roles on both sides of the War. Some think the faction of Lawrence. G. Murphy and James Joseph "J.J." Dolan was on the side of the law; others think the cause of John Henry Tunstall and Alexander McSween was the right one. The truth is: Both sides were wrong because principals of both were confrontational, greedy and stubborn, and practiced "mob law." Those who legally dealt out the law of that time, in Lincoln and its surrounding area as well as in Santa Fe, were no better than the outlaws they were sworn to capture.

Even if I could, I will not attempt to here give an overview of that very complex conflict. Over the past hundred and quarter years, countless articles and books have been written and are still being written about that war and Billy the Kid. It is a popular subject even today and with many far from southeastern New Mexico. If you want to know more about this interesting subject, countless books and essays are available in print, perhaps now even in e-book form, for purchase or to check out of your local library, or to download to your Kindle or smart phone. Some of those adhere closer to facts than others; many are pure fiction, so cautiously choose what you believe.

One (no longer in print) that often did not stay close to fact is a book supposedly written by Sheriff Patrick Garrett, but ghost written by Asmun Upson: *An Authentic Life of Billy the Kid.* The title was actually much longer. That was the first published book about Billy; it and one by Walter Noble Burns—*Saga of Billy the Kid*—and "dime" paperbacks began the international launch of his legend. If you've inherited a first edition of either above-named book or find one in a garage sale, grab a tight hold onto it; it is a valuable antiquarian item. However, modern publications of both of those are available.

Some history books, many of those on my bookshelves, enhanced with photographs include: two books by Englishman Frederick Nolan, *The West of Billy the Kid* and *The Lincoln County War;* John P. Wilson's *Merchants Guns and Money, the Story of Lincoln County and its Wars;* Robert M. Utley*'s Billy the Kid, A Short and Violent Life*; and Bob Boze Bell's *The Illustrated Life and Times of Billy the Kid.* I have met Nolan several times and we have a friend in common,

Morgan Nelson. For history gathering and vacations, Nolan visits the Roswell area at least once a year and is Nelson's houseguest.

Leaving Roswell, we climb out of the Pecos Valley and the terrain becomes more undulating. The further west we travel, the more distinctive become what I call the "rolling hills of Peter Hurd." Traveling through the Hondo Valley, motorists pass by what had been small Hispanic settlements established before the days of the Lincoln County Wars along the Rio Bonito, the Rio Ruidoso and the Rio Hondo. Besides the remaining small settlements, we pass several large ranches and green meadows with grazing cattle.

As we drop down into the Hondo Valley, The highway goes into a steep, winding descent. We pass Riverside, now only a wide spot beside the highway with two buildings—a cafe and a small store or service station—that are, more often than not, vacant. We pass picturesque Tinnie Mercantile, a restaurant nestled among giant cottonwoods. For decades, this large white rambling building with its striking peaked red roofs and bell-tower has been a favorite subject of artists and photographers.

Across from the Mercantile is the old Tinnie cemetery. We stop to take pictures.

Just past Tinnie Mercantile and within the small roadside community of Tinnie is a road that turns right, north, and climbs into the hills to Arabela. On our photo-op trip today, we take that road, Highway NM-368, with the backdrop of the Capitan Mountain that no longer resembles a teepee. It now looms large in the background.

We travel about seventeen miles, climbing into the foothills of the southeastern end of the Capitans, before the road dead-ends just beyond Arabela. I had believed this small rural community was originally called Los Palos (The Sticks), until corrected by a Roswell WebMag reader from California, who had grown up in the area, his family residents of the Hondo for generations. Ernesto said its original name was Las Palas (The Shovels). The small community had a post office from 1901 to 1928. Its last postmaster was a man named Pacheco. We take photos of a large lovely old home, still occupied, and the remains of the Arabela schoolhouse.

At the dead-end, we turn around and return to Tinnie where the road meets Highway 70-380 and we continue our day's journey.

*Old Lincoln Cemetery*

Today, at the highway Y at Hondo, where travelers choose between going to Ruidoso or Lincoln, we now choose the highway that turns right to Lincoln. On the outskirts of Lincoln, we stop to take photos at the old historic Lincoln cemetery. We see some familiar names from Lincoln County War history.

Entering Lincoln, at mile marker 98, we again stop, this time to photograph the historic Ellis Store, built in 1876, which is now a bed and breakfast on well-manicured grounds with an expanse of lawn edged with a fence heavily draped with blooming spirea. Gracious hosts at the Ellis are David and Ginny Vigil. The historic roadside marker says "Ellis & Sons" had fled the commotion in Colfax County and started a store in Lincoln about 1876.

The small town of Lincoln has been preserved and restored back to the era of the Lincoln County Wars. Nestled between the mountainsides in a long narrow river valley, the town's historic storefronts are neatly lined up on either side of the highway. We pass Casa de Patron and the Montaño Store on our left, the Anderson-Freeman Visitors' Center and Museum set back off the highway on our right. Also on our right is the "Torreon, a stone fortification erected by early Hispanic settlers used as a defensive structure to fight Apaches and used by Murphy-Dolan faction during the Lincoln County War."

Across from the Torreon is Iglesia de San Juan Bautista, the small Catholic Church build in 1887. On our right are: the Tunstall Museum, Dr. Wood's House, an adobe ruin, and the Wortley Hotel and Dining Room, which was once owned by Pat Garrett. The Wortley is not always open for customers. Across the highway are: the small Community Church, the old school house and the Murphy-Dolan Store that later served as the courthouse, now a museum. It was from an upstairs room of that building that William H. "Billy the Kid" Bonney shot sheriff's deputy Bell and then Marshal Bob Olinger, to make his famous "final escape."

I have fond memories of camping in a tent encampment with friends in the grassy meadow behind the Iglesia de San Juan Bautista during an Old Lincoln Days event some years ago. The encampment was a Cavalry soldiers' re-enactment. That night, as I lay under the stars in the crisp and fragrant night air, the surrounding mountainsides magnified and echoed the sounds of whinnying horses and, from a neighboring camp, the rat-a-tat-tat of drums and the mournful tunes of a fife. I even heard bagpipes. The current campers were practicing. The ambience transported me back to the era of the nation's Civil War, as well as the civil war in Lincoln County.

The annual New Mexico Heritage Preservation Week is celebrated for a week in May in Lincoln and the surrounding area. According to their brochure, during those days are "live music; chuckwagon cookin' and cowboy storytellin'; arts & crafts demos; a 19th century infantry camp; walking tours; talks about the Lincoln County War characters; BLM walking tours and lectures; Apache traditions, culture and stories; Hispanic forum & panel discussion; three cultures' tour; carriage rides; Fiber Fest; and spinning & weaving demos at La Placita." The brochure suggests that you "walk the same streets as 'Billy' with historian and author, Drew Gomber." Most of the events are free but some have limited seating; call (505)-653-4025 for reservations. Meal and bedtime accommodations are few in Lincoln; the majority of temporary guests stay in nearby Ruidoso.

After we drive through Lincoln, stopping to explore and take photos, we continue to drive west for several miles. A few miles beyond

Lincoln is, on our left or south, the road to Fort Stanton; we take it.

We drive past the Fort Stanton Post Office. Fort Stanton also celebrates New Mexico Heritage Preservation Week. Their brochure says they offer "good family festivities [including] live military re-enactors, storytellers, Apache dancers, Hispanic settlers, good food and good fun" on Sunday from 10 a.m. to 4 p.m. (We returned to Fort Stanton that Sunday and they indeed had a wonderful celebration, with hundreds of people in attendance, many in period costumes. For that one-day event, the entire Fort Stanton complex was open to the public.)

Volunteers of Fort Stanton, Inc., in partnership with the Roswell field office of the Bureau of Land Management, the Lincoln County Historical Society, the Mescalero Apache Nation and the Ruidoso Valley Chamber of Commerce, staff the small portion of Fort Stanton that is usually accessible to the public.

*Fort Stanton Museum, photo taken by Jan Girand*

Normally, the Fort Stanton Museum and Post Office are the only buildings open to the public. The majority of Fort Stanton, owned by the state of New Mexico, is used as a drug rehabilitation center. Therefore, normally, photo-taking opportunities are limited and then only under strict supervision.

A portion of original Fort Stanton is now preserved but is usually off-limits to the general public. That includes the Fort Stanton historic church.

Fort Stanton Inc. is a non-profit organization dedicated to the preservation of this historically valuable property for posterity. Their brochure reads: "Fort Stanton has led a long, interesting and diverse life. From its establishment during the Indian wars and involvement in the Civil War and the Lincoln County War, it served as a military stronghold. Although decommissioned near the end of the 19th century, it continued to function as a federal hospital, then as a state hospital. Today, Fort Stanton is about to change again. This time the cultural and historical heritage will be restored forever!"

Their brochure also reads: "Fort Stanton [was] established May 1855 to control Apaches in the area. [It was] occupied by Confederate forces in August 1861. [It was] reoccupied by Kit Carson and five companies of New Mexico volunteers in October 1862. Fort Stanton brought stability to the area and encouraged settlement of Lincoln County. [It] was a major control factor during the Lincoln County War. [It] was home to Buffalo Soldiers [the famed black regiment who] helped control Apache bands led by Victorio and Geronimo in the 1880s.

"Fort Stanton is associated with several legendary figures, including Billy the Kid, who was incarcerated in the guardhouse; Territorial Governor Lew Wallace who is reputed to have written parts of his novel *Ben Hur* while relaxing in the quiet of the isolated post; and John J. 'Black Jack' Pershing, commander of the American Expeditionary Forces in WWI, who served two tours of duty at the fort in 1887 and 1889."

The brochure goes on to tell visitors: "Fort Stanton was officially abandoned by the Army in 1896, turned into a Merchant Marine tuberculosis hospital by the Public Health Department in 1899; served [more than] 10,000 Merchant Marines with tuberculosis; was an internment camp for the crew of a German Luxury Liner that was scuttled off the coast of Cuba in 1939; Fort Stanton was transferred to the state of New Mexico in 1953; was entered into the State Register of Historic Places in 1973; and entered the State's Most Endangered Buildings list in 1999."

The U.S. Public Health Service Hospital Cemetery, established 1899, and the Merchant Marine Cemetery, are at Fort Stanton. Here are also buried, separately on the far west end of the cemetery, four Germans from the crew of the German luxury liner, subsequently interned at Fort Stanton, where they died.

Fort Stanton Inc. strongly encourages, and seeks, support efforts from the public to preserve and restore this only surviving fort in the state of New Mexico.

After our sojourn in Lincoln and Fort Stanton, we head for home.

# BTK TIMELINE

## Research by Robert Sproull

| | | |
|---|---|---|
| 1859 | Dec. | According to some, the date Catherine McCarty gives birth to Billy; the year, place and father uncertain. Rumored places of birth were: Cincinnati, Ohio; Springfield, Illinois; Limerick, Ireland; plus the states of Indiana, Kansas, New Mexico, Missouri & New York. Billy is named William Henry McCarty. Joseph is Billy's younger or older brother. |
| 1860 | | Location of McCarty family unknown until 1864, then some evidence they resided in Indiana. |
| 1861 | | 1st Lt. L.G. Murphy joins NM Volunteers at Ft. Union. |
| 1862 | 31-Oct | Ft. Sumner established at Bosque Redondo. |
| 1863 | | Michael McCarty of Marion Co., Indiana, dies of battle wounds. Some think he was the father of Billy. |
| 1864 | 1-Nov | L.G. Murphy promoted to major for distinguished service at Adobe Walls under Kit Carson. |
| 1865 | | William Antrim of Indianapolis meets Catherine McCarty, "widow of Michael McCarty." |
| 1866 | 20-Oct | Santa Fe Gazette publishes a letter from L.G. Murphy of Ft. Stanton. Murphy, Fritz, & James Dolan mustered out of the Army. Fritz and Murphy establish a store. |
| 1867 | | John Chisum arrives in New Mexico. Antrim and Catherine thought to be living in Indianapolis near each other. |
| 1868 | | John Chisum establishes a ranch at Bosque Grande. Lucien B Maxwell buys Ft. Sumner, that is, the structures, not the land underneath, which remains U.S. Government property. |
| 1869 | | McCartys in Wichita, Kansas |
| 1870 | | McCartys in Wichita, Kansas. Catron confirmed as Attorney General of NM Territory (on Jan 14) |
| 1871 | | Catherine McCarty sells Wichita holdings. |
| 1872 | | U.S. Post Office established at Rio Hondo. (Now Roswell) |

| | | |
|---|---|---|
| 1873 | 1-Mar | Catherine and William Antrim married in Santa Fe; Billy & brother Joe witness. |
| | Jun | Antrims arrive in Silver City, buy a cabin. Catherine takes in wash, boarders. Billy runs with the "Street Arabs." |
| | Dec | Billy acts in Minstrel shows; "a good singer." |
| | | |
| 1874 | May | Catherine becomes bedridden from her TB. |
| | 16-Sep | Catherine dies of TB. Billy lives with Hudsons and then the Truesdales. Billy's teacher Mary Richards (of England). Mary said to be one of the best educated young ladies in England—perhaps in the world! She knew and/or worked with Disraeli, Ruskin & Tennyson, exchanged letters. |
| | | |
| 1875 | Summer | Truesdales split. Billy sent to live with the Browns. He learns gambling at the Orleans Club. |
| | 4-Sep | Robbery of Charlie Sun (with George Schaffer) |
| | 23-Sep | Arrested and jailed by Sheriff Whitehill. |
| | 25-Sep | Escapes jail through its chimney. |
| | 26-Sep | Gets on stage to Arizona. |
| | | |
| 1876 | 19-Jan | Wm. Rynerson appointed District Attorney for the Third Judicial District of NM Territory, Dona Ana, Grant and Lincoln Counties. |
| | 19-Mar | Young Billy steals a horse from Pvt. Smith, San Carlos Indian Reservation. Goes to Ft. Grant & McDowell's Store. Works at Hooker's Ranch; Hotel de Luna. |
| | Nov. 6 | Tunstall arrives in Lincoln. |
| | Nov | Billy steals a horse from Sgt. Hartman. (Hartman recovers it.) Billy escapes jail several times. |
| | | |
| 1877 | 17-Aug | Kills Frank (Windy) Cahill in a fight. Jailed; indicted for murder. Escapes jail. Goes to Knight's Ranch, Silver City. Reported running with Jesse Evans' gang. Heads to Pecos Valley. Waylaid by Apaches. Gets to Ma'am Jones Ranch, barefooted. Arrested at Seven Rivers. Winter time spent with Frank Coe. |
| | | |
| 1878 | Jan. | Hired by Tunstall. McSween and Tunstall are in competition with the Murphy group. McSween has to post bond for dispute on the Fritz insurance money. |
| | 11-Feb | Sheriff Brady attaches Tunstall Store and cattle for McSween's bond money. |
| | 18-Feb | Tunstall murdered by Brady posse. |
| | 1-Mar | Brewer forms the Regulators. Brewer is made Special Constable by Justice Wilson; Billy appointed Deputy. |
| | 6-Mar | Brewer posse captures Morton and Baker. |
| | 9-Mar | Dolan organizes 70-man party to rescue them |
| | 9-Mar | Morton & Baker killed "attempting to escape." McCloskey also killed. |
| | 1-Apr | Sheriff Brady & Hindeman killed in ambush by Billy and others. |
| | 4-Apr | Buckshot Roberts killed by Regulators at Blazers Mill, Brewer killed. Coe, |

Billy & Middleton wounded.

|  |  |  |
|---|---|---|
| | 6-Apr | Dudley assumes command at Ft. Stanton. |
| | 22-24- | |
| | Apr | Grand Jury exonerates McSween. Dolan and others indicted for Tunstall murder. |
| | | Copeland appointed Sheriff. |
| | 28-Apr | Seven Rivers Gang rides to Lincoln to join fight. |
| | 8-May | Frank Angel arrives in Lincoln as Pres. Hayes representative. |
| | 28-May | Gov. Axtel removes Copeland, appoints Peppin as sheriff. |
| | 18-Jun | Congress passes Posse Comitas Act. |
| | Jul | McSween & regulators are fugitives. |
| | 14-Jul | McSween & others return to Lincoln. Beginning of 5-day Battle. Dudley & Army intervene. |
| | 19-Jul | McSween & others killed fleeing his burning home. Higinio Salazar, Billy, Folliard & French escape. |
| | 20-Jul | Coroners Jury. McSween & others killed "Resisting arrest." |
| | 14-Aug | Billy & others at Paco Anaya's camp. Angel leaves for New York. |
| | Aug-Sep | Kinney & Dona Ana Gang terrorize area. |
| | 4-Sep | Pres Hayes replaces Axtel with Gov. Wallace. |
| | 13-Nov | Wallace issues Amnesty Proclamation. |
| | 22-Dec | Kimbrell replaces Peppin as Sheriff; arrests Billy. Billy escapes. |
| | 28-Dec | Billy meets Jesse James in Las Vegas, NM |
| 1879 | 18-Feb | Peace parley in Lincoln. (Billy & Evan's Gang.) |
| | | Dolan & Evans murder lawyer Chapman. |
| | | Governor will go to Lincoln, wants to capture Billy as a witness to the murder. |
| | 1-Mar | Wallace arrives in Lincoln for one month. |
| | 15-Mar | Wallace writes Billy and suggests a meeting. |
| | 17-Mar | Gov. Wallace and Billy meet in Lincoln. |
| | 18-Mar | Evans & Campbell escape from Ft. Stanton. |
| | | Wallace offers $1000 reward for capture. |
| | 21-Mar | Billy & Folliard surrender as agreed to in the agreement with Wallace. |
| | 14-Apr | Wallace convenes a Grand Jury. Rynerson won't let Billy testify; changes venue to Mesilla. |
| | 25-May | Dudley Court of Inquiry convened. |
| | 28-May | Billy testifies at the Dudley Court of Inquiry. |
| | June | Billy distrusts Wallace; rides away. |
| | 2-Jul | Court of Inquiry exonerates Dudley. |
| | August | Judge Bristol dismisses all charges re Dolan. |
| | 6-Dec | All civil charges against Dudley dismissed by Judge Bristol. |
| 1880 | 10-Jan | Billy kills Joe Grant at Ft. Sumner |
| | 14-Jan | Pat Garrett & Apolonaria Guitierrez wed at Ft. Sumner. |
| | 30-Apr | John Jones & Marion Turner indicted for the murder of McSween. |
| | 20-Jun | Susan McSween marries George Barber. |
| | Oct | Capt. Lee, Chisum & Dolan nominate Pat Garrett for Sheriff. |
| | 2-Nov | Garrett elected Sheriff. Acts as Kimbrell's Deputy until term begins. |
| | 12-Nov | Wallace's novel, BEN HUR, published. |

| | 27-Nov | Carlyle killed at Greathouse; Billy escapes. |
|---|---|---|
| | 12-Dec | Billy writes Wallace protesting his innocence. |
| | 15-Dec | Wallace offers $500 reward for the capture of Billy. Catron sells Murphy store to Lincoln Co. Commissioners for a Courthouse. |
| | 19-Dec | Folliard killed at Ft. Sumner. (Garrett Posse.) |
| | 23-Dec | Billy, Rudabaugh & Wilson captured at Stinking Springs by Garrett. Bowdre killed. |
| | 24-Dec | Billy and gang put in irons at Ft. Sumner. |
| | 25-Dec | Garrett's posse & prisoners have Christmas dinner at Grzelachowski's Roadhouse. |
| | 26-Dec | Prisoners delivered to Las Vegas jail. Wallace leaves for the East Coast. |
| | 27-Dec | Billy & Gang delivered to Santa Fe Jail. |
| 1881 | 1-Jan | Billy writes letter to Gov. Wallace. |
| | 28-Feb | Billy & companions caught trying to dig out. |
| | 2-Mar | Billy writes second letter to Gov. Wallace. |
| | 4-Mar | Billy writes third letter to Gov. Wallace. |
| | 9-Mar | Wallace offers resignation to Pres. Garfield. |
| | 17-Mar | Garfield accepts Wallace's resignation. |
| | 27-Mar | Billy writes final letter to Gov. Wallace. |
| | 6-Apr | Murder of Buckshot Roberts by Billy quashed. |
| | 9-Apr | Billy found guilty of the murder of Sheriff Brady. |
| | 13-Apr | Billy sentenced to be hanged on May 13. |
| | 21-Apr | Billy jailed in Lincoln County Courthouse to await hanging on May 13. |
| | 28-Apr | Billy kills guards Bell & Olinger and escapes. He goes to Las Tablas & Higinio Salazar. Gets horse from the Block Ranch and goes to Ft. Sumner area. |
| | 30-Apr | Gov. Wallace offers $500 reward for Billy. Earlier in day he had signed Billy's death warrant. |
| | May/June | Billy spends time going from sheep ranch to sheep ranch. Attends dances, gambles. He won't go to Mexico. |
| | 14-Jul | Garrett kills Billy in Pete Maxwell's bedroom. |

# 1859 to 1881 TIMELINE
## Of World & National Events
## To Compare with Billy's Timeline

### Research by Robert Sproull

| 1859 | 14-Feb | Oregon admitted as 33rd state. |
|---|---|---|
| | 27-Aug | Col. Drake drills the world's first oil well. Titusville, Pa. |
| | 16-Oct | John Brown raids Harper's Ferry, Virginia. |
| | 2-Dec | John Brown hung for his raid. |
| | All year | Forty-niners stream into Rocky Mountains during the 1859 Gold Rush. |
| 1860 | 3-Apr | Pony Express, St. Joseph, Mo. to Sacramento, begun. |

| | | |
|---|---|---|
| | 3-Nov | Abraham Lincoln elected as 16th U.S. President. |
| | 20-Dec | South Carolina secedes from the Union. |
| | | |
| 1861 | Jan | Mississippi, Florida, Alabama, Georgia, Louisiana secede. Kansas admitted as a state. |
| | 1-Feb | Texas secedes from the Union. |
| | 4-Mar | President Lincoln inaugurated. |
| | 12-Apr | Ft. Sumter attacked. Civil War Begins. |
| | 27-Apr | West Virginia secedes from Virginia. |
| | May | Arkansas, Tennessee and North Carolina secede. |
| | Nov | Jefferson Davis elected president of the Confederacy. |
| | | |
| 1862 | Jan-Dec | Civil War (1861-1865) continues. |
| | 5-May | Cinco de Mayo. Mexicans defeat the French at Pueblo. |
| | 9-May | Richard Gatling patented his machine gun. |
| | 15-May | Lincoln signs the Homestead Act. |
| | | |
| 1863 | Jan-Dec | Civil War (1861-1865) continues. |
| | 1-Jan | Lincoln Signs the Emancipation Proclamation. |
| | 10-Feb | General Tom Thumb and Lavinia Warren married. |
| | Jul 1-3 | Battle of Gettysburg. |
| | 5-Oct | The Brooklyn, Bath & Coney Island Railroad opens. |
| | 15-Oct | First successful submarine (CSS Hunley) sinks. |
| | | |
| 1864 | Jan-Dec | Civil War (1861-1865) continues. |
| | 10-Apr | Maximilian proclaimed Emperor of Mexico. |
| | 22-Apr | "In God We Trust" placed on US currency by Congress. |
| | 8-Nov | Lincoln re-elected over McClellan. |
| | | |
| 1865 | 4-Mar | Lincoln inaugurated for his second term. |
| | 9-Apr | Lee surrenders to Grant at Appomattox. |
| | 14-Apr | Lincoln shot at Ford's Theatre. |
| | 15-Apr | Lincoln dies. Andrew Johnson sworn in. (17th Pres.) |
| | 13-May | Battle of Palmito Ranch, TX. Last battle of Civil War. |
| | 2-Jun | Civil War Ends. |
| | | |
| 1866 | 10-Apr | ASPCA founded in NYC. |
| | 16-May | Charles Hires invents root beer. |
| | 27-Jul | Atlantic Cable completed. |
| | 21-Dec | Fetterman Massacre. Sioux wipe out 79 cavalrymen. |
| | | |
| 1867 | 8-Jan | Benito Juarez again becomes Mexican President. |
| | 16-Mar | Lister's "Antiseptic surgery" published. |
| | 30-Mar | "Seward's Folly;" Alaska purchased for $7.2 million. |
| | Jun | Lucien Smith's "Barbed Wire" patented. (Called "rotary spools w/ projecting spurs.") |

| | 19-Jun | Firing squad executes Maximilian of Mexico. |
| | 17-Jul | Harvard establishes first U.S. Dental School. |

| 1868 | 16-May | President Johnson acquitted, impeachment trial over his dismissal of Secretary of War Stanton |
| | 30-May | First Memorial Day celebration. |
| | 28-Oct | Thomas Edison applies for his first patent. (The Electric Vote Recorder.) |
| | 25-Dec | President Johnson grants unconditional pardon to all Civil War rebels. |

| 1869 | 14-Jan | Catron confirmed as NM Attorney General. |
| | 4-Mar | Ulysses S. Grant inaugurated as President of the U.S. |
| | 10-May | Transcontinental Railroad completed, Promontory, Utah. |
| | 31-Aug | Mary Ward killed in an auto accident! (And autos not yet been patented!) |
| | 17-Nov | Suez Canal is inaugurated. |

| 1870 | | Railroads and expanded markets bring flood of buffalo hunters to the plains. Buffalo endangered species in 10 years. Advertising brings floods of settlers to the West. |
| | 10-Jan | John D. Rockefeller incorporates Standard Oil. |
| | 15-Jan | Nast's political cartoon creates the Democrat's Donkey. |
| | 28-Jan | Maxwell Land Grant sold for $1.3 million. |
| | 30-Mar | Texas readmitted to the Union. |
| | 24-May | Opening day of the Brooklyn Bridge. |
| | 17-Jul | Beginning of the Franco-Prussian War |

| 1871 | 4-May | First Major League baseball game is played. |
| | 8-10-Oct | Great Chicago Fire. |
| | 17-Nov | National Rifle Association granted a Charter. (NY State) |

| 1872 | 10-May | End of Franco-Prussian War. |
| | 1-Mar | Yellowstone National Park established. (World's first.) |
| | 5-Nov | Susan B. Anthony votes, is arrested & fined. Won't pay. |
| | 21-Dec | HMS Challenger sails from Portsmouth; a 4 year voyage. This laid the foundation for oceanography. |

| 1873 | 15-Mar | President Grant begins his second term of office. |
| | 21-Jul | Jesse James & gang. First successful train robbery in the American West at Adair, Iowa. |
| | 18-Sep | NY stock market crash triggers panic of 1873. Long depression. |
| | 15-Dec | WCTU got its start in the march of Fredonia, NY ladies. |

| 1874 | 20-May | Levi Strauss. US patent for copper rivets on jeans. |
| | 7-Nov | Nast cartoon; Elephant as symbol of Republican Party. |
| | 24-Nov | Thomas Glidden receives a patent for barbed wire. |
| | 30-Nov | Winston Churchill born. |

| 1875 | 17-May | Aristides wins the first Kentucky Derby. Time: 2:37 ¾. |
| | 1-Sep | "Molly Maguires" disbanded. (Cause: murder conviction.) |
| | 9-Nov | Indian Inspector Watkins warns that the Sioux and Cheyenne are hostile to the United States. |
| | | |
| 1876 | 31-Jan | US orders all Native Americans to move to reservations. |
| | 7-Mar | Bell granted patent for the telephone. |
| | 15-May | Vagrant wins Kentucky Derby. Time: 2:38 ¼. |
| | 25-Jun | Battle of the Little Big Horn; Custer and his troops lose. |
| | 4-Jul | The United States celebrates its Centennial. |
| | 7-Nov | Hayes vs. Tilden presidential election. Hayes finally declared winner. |
| | 29-Nov | Porfirio Diaz becomes President of Mexico. |
| | | |
| 1877 | 8-Jan | Crazy Horse defeated by the U.S. Cavalry. |
| | 2-Mar | Compromise of 1877. Hayes declared the winner even though Tilden won popular vote. Haynes had more Electoral College votes and, Per the Constitution, becomes president. |
| | 4-Mar | Rutherford B. Hayes becomes President of the US. |
| | 22-May | Baden-Baden wins Kentucky Derby. Time: 2:38. |
| | 21-Nov | Edison invents the phonograph; his 1st great invention. |
| | | |
| 1878 | Jan | Cleopatra's Needle arrives in London. |
| | 6-Jan | Carl Sandburg, American poet, is born. (Died 1967) |
| | 11-Feb | First US bicycle club forms in Boston. |
| | 19-Feb | The phonograph is patented by Edison. |
| | 13-Mar | Oxford defeats Cambridge in their 1st golf match. |
| | 10-Apr | California Street Cable Car RR Co. starts service. |
| | 12-Apr | "Boss" William Tweed, NY politician, dies |
| | 15-Apr | Marley Proctor introduces Ivory Soap. |
| | 14-May | Vaseline first sold. |
| | 22-May | Day Star wins Kentucky Derby. Time: 2:37 ¼. |
| | 25-May | Gilbert & Sullivan "HMS Pinafore" premiers in London. |
| | 20-Jul | 1st Telephone introduced in Hawaii. |
| | 12-Sep | Cleopatra's Needle installed in London. |
| | 17-Oct | The Edison Electric Company begins operation |
| | 1-Dec | 1st White House Telephone installed. |
| | 26-Dec | 1st US store to install electric lights, Philadelphia |
| | | |
| 1879 | | Cleveland and San Francisco install street lighting by electricity. |
| | 15-Feb | Pres. Hayes signs bill permitting female attorneys to argue cases before the Supreme Court. |
| | 27-Feb | Woolworth opens his first 5 & 10 in Utica, NY. |
| | 8-May | Selden files for a patent on an internal combustion engine road vehicle. |
| | 20-May | Lord Murphy wins Kentucky Derby. Time: 2:37. |
| | 25-May | St. Patrick's Cathedral in NY is dedicated. |
| | 19-Jul | Doc Holliday kills his first man, in Las Vegas, NM saloon |

| | Sep | Carlisle Training & Industrial School for Indians founded |
| | 24-Oct | Edison tests the first practical light bulb. |
| | | |
| 1880 | 2-Feb | First electric streetlight is installed in Wabash, Ind. |
| | 9-Feb | First locomotive arrives in Santa Fe. |
| | 6-Apr | Victorio's warriors & Hatch's troopers have battle in Hembrillo Canyon near Tularosa. |
| | 18-May | Fonso wins Kentucky Derby. Time: 2:37 ½. |
| | Oct | Terrible winter; "Blizzard of 1880." |
| | 15-Oct | Mexican soldiers kill Victorio, greatest Apache military strategist. (Tres Castillos, Mexico.) |
| | 4-Nov | National Cash Register gets patent for their device. |
| | Date? | President Hayes vetoes the Chinese Exclusion Act. |
| | | |
| 1881 | | |
| | 25-Jan | Edison and Bell form the Oriental Telephone Co. |
| | 5-Feb | Phoenix, AZ is incorporated. |
| | 19-Feb | Kansas prohibits all alcohol. (1st State to do so) |
| | 4-Mar | Garfield sworn in as US President. |
| | 14-Apr | "Four Dead in Five Seconds Gunfight". El Paso, TX. |
| | 28-Apr | Billy the Kid escapes from Lincoln Co. Courthouse. Makes news headlines worldwide. |
| | 17-May | Hindoo wins Kentucky Derby. Time: 2:40. |
| | 2-Jul | James A. Garfield shot by Charles Guiteau, a lawyer. Survives but dies of infection. Sep. 19 |
| | 14-Jul | Bastille Day in France. |
| | 14-Jul | Billy the Kid killed by Pat Garrett. Death noted world-wide. |

## Historical Grave Markers in Several Cemeteries
## And their genealogical histories by Charles O. Sanders

### "Find A Grave" Listings:

At <u>CIMARRON</u>: (family burials on Maxwell family property, near their home):
Beaubien, Pabla –1811 to 1864          mother of Luz Beaubien Maxwell
Maxwell, Verenisa –1860 to 1864          child of Luz & Lucien Maxwell

*Graves of Verenisa Maxwell, age about 3, and her grandmother Maria Pabla Beaubien, age 53; both died in 1864.  Photo by Jan Girand*

Graves of Verenisa Maxwell (1860-1864) and her maternal grandmother, Maria Pabla Beaubien (1811-1864) were located behind the Lucien Maxwell's family home at Cimarron. The large two-story Maxwell Ranché building partly burned in 1888 and the rest was destroyed by fire in 1924. Although the original Maxwell home is gone, the gravesites, encased in cement and encircled by a wrought-iron fence, remain. Pabla was the wife of one of the two original land grantees, Charles Beaubien (1800-1864).

After the death of their daughter, Verenisa, in her memory Lucien and Luz Maxwell built the Immaculate Conception Church in Cimarron in 1864. Jean Baptiste Lamy, Santa Fe's first bishop, dedicated it, which began as a mission church. It was enlarged in 1909 and the new bell and bell-tower were dedicated the next year.

**CIMARRON COMMUNITY CEMETERY, Colfax County NM:**
Lambert, Henri –Oct. 28, 1838 to Jan. 24, 1913 (St. James Hotel in Cimarron)
Lambert, Charles Fred—Oct. 23, 1887 to Feb. 1971 (Henri's son, one of NM's first Mounties)

**ABREU CEMETERY near Rayado, Colfax County, New Mexico**
Abreu, Adelina—July 14, 1866 to Oct. 27, 1867
Abreu, Charley—May 1882 to June 12, 1885
Abreu, Eduardo—April 2, 1882 to Oct. 27, 1882
Abreu, Gertrude Brown—May 23, 1886 to Nov. 13, 1958
Abreu, Jesus G.—Sept. 1, 1823 to June 30, 1900
Abreu, Juanita—March 10, 1874 to Aug. 5, 1874
Abreu, Miguel—Unknown       /       Unknown
Abreu, Narciso—March 22, 1921 to Oct. 8, 1990
Abreu, Pablo—Unknown       / Unknown
Abreu, Petra Beaubien—June 29, 1844 to July 4, 1914
Abreu, Philip Narciso—May 29, 1926 to Feb. 5, 1953
Abreu, Ramon—March 26, 1880 to Oct. 15, 1882
Abreu, Ramon Eduardo—March 2, 1885 to Feb. 22, 1928
Abreu, Raymond E.—April 11 __ to March 14, 1995
Abreu, Sofia—Feb. 18, 1872 to Nov. 1, 1917
*There were additional listed non-Abreu burials there, perhaps family servants, etc.*

**Below, "quote marks" signify inscriptions on the stones. [Brackets] signify genealogy information relating to these persons, provided by Charles O. Sanders**

<u>**In old Cemetery at Lincoln New Mexico:**</u>

## Yginio Salazar, Pal of Billy the Kid
### Research by Charles O. Sanders

"Billy's Pal" Yginio Salazar's modern grave marker in the Lincoln County Cemetery. The original was probably a wooden marker, long gone. Inscription on this stone:

| | |
|---|---|
| YGINIO SALAZAR | ISABEL SALAZAR |
| BORN | BORN |
| FEB. 14, 1863 | SEPT. 3, 1868 |
| DIED | DIED |
| JAN. 7, 1936 | MAY 15, 1935 |
| PAL OF BILLY THE KID | |

According to another marker, under the same cement slab (also?) lies the remains of "Francisco Salazar" with the dates: 29 Jan 1868 – 5 Sep 1935. Because the name, birth and death dates are the same, apparently he was Francisco Bonney Salazar, husband of Sara Baca, the son of Bernardo Salazar and Maria Rafaela Bonney.

This Yginio and Isabel Salazar marker has incorrect dates of birth. On 3 July 1860, the U.S. census-taker recorded Higinio Salazar as a 3 years old child in his parents' home. The 1870 census shows Yginio Salazar was 11; in 1880, he was 21; in 1900 he was 41, born February 1859; in 1910 he was 50; in 1920 he was 66; in 1930 he was 70. Therefore, Yginio was born before 1860, maybe 3 years earlier.

Isabel was also born earlier than indicated on the stone. The abstract of Isabel's baptismal/christening record shows she was christened on 21 Jun 1864 at "Our Lady Of The Immaculate Conception, Tomé, Valencia, New Mexico," and her parents were recorded as Luis Paniague and Maria los Angeles Chavez.

A period news clip said Isabel's father, Luis Paniague, was killed by Indians in June 1870. Afterward, his widow, Maria de los Angeles Chavez/Chaves, married Jose Maria Montoya. They had a daughter, Librada Montoya who married Matias Carabajal – and they in turn had a son named Isidro Carabajal who was born 10 Apr 1899 and christened 1 May 1899 in the Santa Rita Catholic Church, Lincoln Co., NM, and Isidro's godparents were recorded as "Iginio Salazar and Isabel Paneague."

In the Santa Fe New Mexican, dated Sunday June 14, 1970, "Looking Back" 100 years ago, it describes a large party of Indians, believed to be Navajo, killed "two worthy citizens, who were out hunting, named Luis Paniague and Jose Garcia." That piece also said the previous day three of those Indians "rode up to within three or four hundred yards of the Brewery belonging to Messrs. Murphy and Fritz, but owing to the number of persons there, left without committing any depredations."

### Old Silver City Cemetery
"Mrs. Katherine Antrim, 1829-1874. Mother of Billy the Kid." This modern headstone—with her name misspelled—commemorates the resting place of Billy's mother, Catherine Antrim, in the old pioneer Silver City Cemetery, Memory Lane.
*http://www.rootsweb.ancestry.com/~nma/grant/history_memorylane.htm*

### Markers In old Cemetery at Fort Sumner, as noted and listed by editor, Jan Girand, in June 2010, research by Charles O. Sanders.

### "Luz B. Maxwell"
[Maria de Luz Beaubien – 24 Jun 1829 – 13 Jul 1900; wife of Lucien Bonaparte Maxwell and daughter of Charles/Carlos Hipolye Trotier Sieur de Beaubien and Maria Paula Lovato]

## "Julian Maxwell"

[Julian Maxwell – Fred Nolan writes the following in *Tascosa: Its Life and Gaudy Times*: "During their stopover, Hoyt was asked to render medical assistance to a young man he remembered as William Maxwell, 'the eldest son of the family [whom he found] dying with a severe case of malignant smallpox for which nothing could be done.' In fact, the eldest son of the Maxwell family was Peter, then twenty-nine. 'William' was a half-Cheyenne adopted by Maxwell and known to the family as Julian; he was just twenty when he died."

Per Charles Sanders: "Hoyt's imagination rivaled that of Jack Meyers Potter, the 'Lead Steer.' I don't know if the Julian Maxwell buried in Fort Sumner is Lucien's adopted son or not. I am reasonably certain that his adopted son was born William New Jr., a son of William New born about 1802 in Illinois and whose death at the hands of Apaches is described below as narrated by Kit Carson. In the 1850 census, William New and family (Jr. not yet born) was recorded three doors from Lucien Maxwell, who in turn was next-door to Kit Carson. In 1860, after William New Sr.'s death, "William New," age 4, was recorded in Lucien Maxwell's family immediately following Maxwell's then youngest daughter, Sofia, also age 4. In Lucien Maxwell's 1870 family, "William Maxwell," age 13, is recorded, again immediately after Sofia and just before Pablita/Paulita. So the odds are very good that William New was Lucien's adopted son. It's possible his middle name was Julian. I doubt he was 'a half-Cheyenne.' The following excerpt is Kit Carson's narration of the death of who was surely his [William New Jr's] biological father, William New: Excerpt from: *The Life and Adventures of Kit Carson, the Nestor of the Rocky Mountains, from Facts Narrated by Himself* - by De Witt C. Peters: "The other person referred to as having been since killed by this tribe of Apaches was a brave and experienced trapper, well known throughout the range of Indian depredations as a fearless and dangerous adversary. His name was William New. He was literally murdered at Rayado by these Apaches. This occurred only a few months after he had formed one of the party to pursue and recover the animals stolen from their ranché. When he was attacked, New was engaged tilling the soil on his own farm. The rascally Indians surrounded him before he became aware of their presence. Having an empty rifle with him, he succeeded, for some time, in keeping his assailants at bay, by pretending that the piece was loaded and pointing it at the foremost warrior as if he intended to fire it. The savages, however, finally discovered the truth and immediately made a rush upon him. A most desperate fight ensued, for William New, even thus defenceless [sic], was not one who would yield up his life without a struggle. He made almost superhuman efforts to effect his escape, using the rifle as a club; wound after wound was given him in rapid succession in return for the desperate blows which he dealt with the rifle. His efforts, however, proved futile. Gradually the red blood was gathered from his body and drank up by the soil to which he looked for the sustenance of himself and family, until finally, he sank upon the ground fainting from its loss, literally covered from head to foot with frightful wounds. Thus died one more of the sparse race of original mountaineers, now fast passing away, bravely meeting the fate that has hitherto usually awaited this band of fearless men."]

## "Pablita Jaramillo"

[Pablita Jaramillo – better known as Paulita Maxwell (Jan 1864 – 17 Dec 1929) daughter of Lucien Bonaparte Maxwell and Maria de Luz Beaubien. Her husband (later divorced) was Jose Felix Jaramillo (May 1862 – 27 Mar 1937). They were married 14 Jan 1883.]

## "Joseph Nalda June 26, 1937 – June 30, 1938"

[Joseph Nalda – son of Frenchman, Michel Nalda and Maria Soledad Abreu—daughter of Manuel L. Abreu and OdilaVerenisa Maxwell. Manuel L. Abreu was the brother of Rebecca Abreu, wife of Juan Cristobal Pablo Beaubien, kid brother of Lucien Maxwell's wife Luz Beaubien. Manuel and Rebecca Abreu were the children of Henry Maken and Maria Soledad Abreu, sister of Jose de Jesus Gil Abreu, children of former Governor Santiago Abreu. Odila Verenisa Maxwell was Manuel L. Abreu's 2nd wife, after death of his first wife. His 1st wife was Odila's sister, Emilia Maxwell – both daughters of Lucien Maxwell and Luz Beaubien.]

## "Pablo Beaubien 1849—1903"

[Pablo Beaubien - Juan Cristobal Pablo Beaubien (Jul 1848 – 1903), husband of Rebecca Abreu, the kid brother of Lucien Maxwell's wife Luz Beaubien, both children of Charles/Carlos Beaubien and Maria Paula Lovato.]

"Rebecca A. Beaubien 1855—1932"
[Rebecca A. Beaubien - Rebecca Abreu (Aug 1856 – 1 Mar 1933), wife of Juan Cristobal Pablo Beaubien and sister of Manuel L. Abreu who married Emilia and Odila Verenisa Maxwell. Rebecca Abreu and her brother, Manuel, were the children of Henry Maken and Maria Soledad Abreu, sister of Jose de Jesus Gil Abreu. Maria Soledad Abreu and Jose de Jesus Gil Abreu were the children of former Governor Santiago Abreu.]

"Paul C. Beaubien 1893—1929"
[Paul C. Beaubien – Pablo C. Beaubien (16 Dec 1893 – 11 Feb 1929), son of Juan Cristobal Pablo Beaubien and Rebecca Abreu.]

"Peter Maxwell Born April 27, 1848, Died June 21, 1898"
Peter Maxwell's grave is a mound covered with cement, surrounded by a snug-fitting wrought-iron fence. An inscription on marker: "No Pain, No ____" (*PastWord Editor unable to read rest of inscription.*)

Large headstone with name "Abreu." Names listed below on it:
"Manuel Sr."
[Manuel L. Abreu (Jun 1857 – 12 Jul 1925) Husband of Emilia and Odila Verenisa Maxwell.]
"Odila M."
[Odila Verenisa Maxwell (25 Jul 1869 – 5 May 1935) 2nd wife of Manuel L. Abreu.]
"Emelia M."
[Emilia Maxwell (Oct 1852 – 1884) 1st wife of Manuel L. Abreu.]
"Manuel Jr."
[Presumably Manuel Francisco Abreu (18 Sep 1898 – 26 Mar 1940), son of Manuel L. Abreu and Odila Verenisa Maxwell. This Manuel Francisco Abreu is definitely the Manuel 'Mannie' Abreu with his own marker below.]
"Alfredo"
[Alfredo 'Fred' Napoleon Bonaparte Abreu (1 May 1894 – Sep 1952) son of Manuel L. Abreu and OdilaVerenisa Maxwell.]
"Luz"
[Luz Abreu (Aug 1890 – 31 May 1936) daughter ofManuel L. Abreu and Odila Verenisa Maxwell.
"Enriques"
[?]
"Amalia"
[?]
On a separate marker:
"Manuel Abreu 'Mannie' born Sept. 18, 1898, died March 26, 1940"
[Manuel Francisco Abreu (18 Sep 1898 – 26 Mar 1940) son of Manuel L. Abreu and Odila Verenisa Maxwell.]

"Charlie Foor Dec. 12, 1850 –Jan. 20, 1940 Early Settler Came to NM 1880"
[Charles Wesley Foor – born either 8 Dec 1850 or 12 Dec 1850 in Meade Co., Kentucky. An abstract of his death certificate records his death as 3 Jan 1940. According to his 1907 bio by George B. Anderson, Charles Wesley Foor "came to New Mexico in 1881, arriving at Fort Sumner on the 29th of October ..."]

"Siberia Beaubien Foor wife of Charles Foor, raised by Indians, mother of 8"
[Siberia Beaubien Foor – Sieberia Beaubien (born Jul 1868 – died before 1920). The "raised by Indians" on the stone would seem to be a half-truth at best. Her father was Juan Candelario Beaubien, recorded as

baptized 3 Feb 1846, "1 day old, natural son of Maria Soledad Beaubien, family of Don Carlos Beaubien and Dona Maria Paula Lovato. Baptized by Padre Antonio Jose Martínez. Maria Soledad was of the family of Carlos Beaubien and Maria Paula Lobato of la Plaza de Nuestra Senora de Guadelupe de Taos. Baptism Godparents: Pedro Antonio Valdez and Maria Paula Lobato." Juan Candelario Beaubien's mother, recorded baptized 5 Nov 1845 as "Maria Soledad, age abt 20 years of the Ute tribe, family of Carlos Beaubien and Paula Lovato."

As to who raised who and when – Sieberia's father, Juan Candelario Beaubien, was raised in the family of Carlos Beaubien and Maria Paula Lovato until they both died in 1864. His mother, Maria Soledad Beaubien, "Indian servant of Don Carlos Beaubien," had died 21 Aug 1854. After the deaths of Carlos Beaubien and Maria Paula Lovato, he lived in the family of Maria Leonora de los Dolores Beaubien, daughter of the deceased Carlos and Paula. Also in Leonora's family was Maria Alvina Trujillo, born about 1853, the apparent daughter of Leonora Beaubien and Vidal Epimenio Trujillo who married 25 Aug 1845 and divorced 3 Apr 1865. On 19 Nov 1869, Juan Candelario Beaubien and Maria Alvina Trujillo were married, "Without conducting the usual practices and for grave motives." Fray Guerin married Juan and Maria Alvina, both raised by Lenora Beaubien (daughter of Carlos). Godparents: Nester Martinez and Rita Valdez. In 1870, Juan Candelario Beaubien, wife Maria Alvina Trujillo, and their two-year-old daughter, Sieberia, were still living within the family of Leonora Beaubien, who by then was divorced again (this time from Barney J. Oneal). In 1880, Sieberia was still with her parents Juan Candelario Beaubien (who died 24 Nov 1920) and Maria Alvina Trujillo (who died between 1910 and 1920). Sieberia married John Wesley Foor 29 Nov 1884. Therefore, the only Indian who raised Sieberia would seem to be her natural father, Juan Candelario Beaubien, who, reading between the lines in the censuses, was probably only half-Indian, through his mother. ]

"Sandovals" (surrounded by a fence):
"Isaac Sandoval 1862 – 1933"
[Isaac Sandoval - Isaac Aragon Sandoval (22 May 1862 - 1933) son of Ezequiel Guiterrez Sandoval and Maria Dolores Aragon.]
"Victoria Sandoval 1874 – 1916"
[Victoria Sandoval - Victoriana Griego, 2nd wife of Isaac Aragon Sandoval – and daughter of Isidro Griego and Irinea Segura, sister of Alejandro Segura, Justice of the Peace, who served on the Milnor Rudulph Coroner's Jury.]
"Celestino Sandoval May 9, 1867 Died 1950 recuerdo de su esposa hijo … nietos."
[Celestino Sandoval - Jose Celestino Sandoval (19 May 1867 - 2 Dec 1950) brother of Isaac Aragon Sandoval, both sons of Ezequiel Guiterrez Sandoval and Maria Dolores Aragon.]

"Maggie S. Silva 1896—1922"
[Maggie S. Silva – Margaret "Maggie" Spitz (Jan 1896 - 16 May 1922) wife of Jesus Cenovio Silva— parents of Luciano Frank "Chano" Silva. Maggie Spitz was a daughter of William F. Spitz and Maria Lucinda Garcia who was a daughter of Nepomuceno Garcia and Francisca Segura, sister of Alejandro Segura, Justice of the Peace, who served on the Milnor Rudulph Coroner's Jury.]

"Jesus Silva" (no other info on stone) (* See his obit further below.)
[Jesus Silva - Jesus Cenovio Silva (30 Oct 1873 - 4 May 1940) husband of Margaret "Maggie" Spitz, parents of Luciano Frank "Chano" Silva. Jesus Cenovio Silva was a son of Jesus Maria Silva and Cesaria Marez. An Old Fort Sumner Cemetery list prepared by Don McAlvy in 1997 states that "In the St. Anthony's cemetery in old part of Ft. Sumner are the graves of Jesus Silva and his wife. Jesus was Billy the Kid's friend and credited with digging his grave, died at age 98 in 1940. Both his and his wife's markers were stolen." This Jesus Silva and his wife were Jesus Cenovio Silva's parents, Jesus Maria Silva and Cesaria Marez. Jesus Maria Silva was born (according to his obit) 13 Oct 1853 and died 30 May 1941 at the

age of 87 (that according to his obit and death certificate abstract). His wife, Cesaria Marez, died 14 Mar 1934.]

"Luciano Frank Silva PFC US Marine Corp. Dec. 20, 1918—May 26, 2004 purple heart"
[Luciano Frank Silva - Luciano Frank "Chano" Silva (20 Dec 1918 - 26 May 2004) husband of Lois Pena, and son of Jesus Cenovio Silva and Margaret "Maggie" Spitz. Chano's uncle and aunt—his father's brother, Francisco "Frank" Silva, and his wife, Luz Spitz, his mother's sister—raised him. A note on Don McAlvy's Old Fort Sumner Cemetery list states: "L. F. "Chano" Silva, age 80, still living in February 1998, has erected his headstone next to his father and mother. Chano claims he will be the last buried in this old military cemetery as he has a court order saying so!" Chano served in the U.S. Marines in the Pacific in WWII, wounded at Okinawa, Ryukyu Islands on 7 May 1945.]

"Christian Palmer born Dec. 10, 1900 – died July 3, 1902"
[Christian Palmer – last of five children born to Braxton Bragg Palmer and Cecelia Trujillo. Christian was the only one who died in infancy. His father, Braxton, was born 10 Apr 1862 in Cooke Co., TX. Cecelia Trujillo was born 4 Jun 1875 in Fort Sumner, daughter of Cruz Trujillo who was son of Jose Miguel Trujillo and Maria Antonia Valdes. In 1910 census, Braxton Bragg Palmer was recorded as a Saloon Keeper in Fort Sumner.]

"Juanita Gonzales   Mar. 1884 – April 11, 1940"
"Rumaldo Gonzales   Mar. 1875—Jan. 17, 1925"
[Death certificate abstract for a Romualdo Gonzales, born 7 Feb 1876, died 18 Jan 1925, and buried in "Old Fort Sumner Cemetery on 19 Jan 1925." His wife is recorded as Juanita S. Gonzales on that certificate. There is also a death certificate abstract for a widow Juanita Gonzales who died in Fort Sumner 11 Jul 1940 at age 56, with her parents recorded as Donciano Segura.]

Amarillo Daily News (Amarillo, Texas) 1941 June 3 (Tuesday)
Finder of The Kid's Body Dies
"CLOVIS, June 2 - Jesus Maria Silva, 87, a pioneer of Billy the Kid days at Ft. Sumner, died Friday night at the home of his daughter-in-law, Mrs. Frank Silva, in the river town. Funeral services were held at the Catholic Church in Ft. Sumner Saturday.
Silva was born Oct. 13, 1853, at Bernalillo, and went to Ft. Sumner when he was 20 years old. Silva was one of only a few men left who knew The Kid personally. He was the last to talk to Billy before he walked unwittingly into the trap in Maxwell's bedroom where Sheriff Pat Garrett shot The Kid.
Silva told a Clovis News-Journal reporter several years ago that he was standing under a tree near the palacious [sic] Maxwell home that night when Billy the Kid walked up and engaged in conversation for a few minutes.
'Billy,' he said, 'walked on over to Maxwell's house and entered Maxwell's bedroom. A moment later there were gunshots and I rushed over there. The room was dark. I went in and Billy was lying on the floor, a long meat knife in one hand and his gun in the other. He was dead.'
Silva told of helping to remove The Kid's body to a carpenter shop nearby where they placed the body on a carpenter's bench. There it was dressed for burial the next morning, he said.
Silva, blind at the end, had a vivid memory of those colorful days of the early 1880s at Ft. Sumner. At that time he was a young man of prominence in his community and his acquaintanceship with The Kid and the latter's life was unquestioned by those who wrote of The Kid's wild exploits."

Editor's Note: Silva claimed Billy had a gun in his hand, while other witnesses said he was unarmed except for a butcher knife. It is widely believed that Billy's purpose for being near Maxwell's bedroom that night was to cut a piece of meat from a nearby hanging beef for someone to cook for him because he was hungry.

Also note that Silva said Billy's body was laid on a carpenter's bench in another building, while other witnesses do not mention him being taken to a nearby carpenter's shop or laid upon a bench there.

Fort Sumner was established in 1862 by Congress as a military fort to protect settlers of the Pecos River Valley from Indian attacks. Also established was the Bosque Redondo, a reservation where 9,000 Navajo and Apache Indians were confined together. When it was known as a failure and closed by the U.S. Government, in 1869 Lucien Maxwell bought the property (but not the land it sat upon) and rebuilt one of the officers' quarters into this (above) 20-room dwelling for his family, including his son, Pete "Pedro," and daughter, Paulita, who continued to live there after his death. It was in Pete's corner bedroom that opened directly off the wrap-around porch, that Sheriff Patrick Garrett shot and killed Billy "the Kid" Bonney.

## Don Martín Cháves of Picacho
### As told by District Judge Freddie Romero,
### With input from Phelps Anderson,
### to Jan Girand

The Martín Cháves home, above recent photo courtesy Phelps Anderson, had become part of Robert O. Anderson's Circle Diamond and Diamond A Ranches in Lincoln County, New Mexico. Mr. Anderson completed restoration of the Martín Cháves home in the 1970s. The Anderson family owns the Cháves home and surrounding farm and ranch lands.

Martín Cháves of Picacho is a familiar name in Lincoln County history, especially as respects the Lincoln County War.

Martín Cháves, respectfully called Don Martín by those who personally knew him and by descendents of those families, was born in 1850 in the small Hispanic settlement of Manzano, situated high in the Manzano Mountains in what is now Torrance County, New Mexico. The Manzanos are southeast of Albuquerque, south of the Sandia Mountains. That community and the mountains that contain it were so-named for ancient apple orchards predating the settlement, possibly planted there by early Indians. They are believed to be some of the oldest apple orchards in America. The Manzano community was settled in 1829.

In 1863, a group of Manzano settlers petitioned the U.S. Surveyor General for dispensation to resettle in the Picacho area of Lincoln County in the southeastern portion of the Territory of New Mexico. No record shows that was the year they settled there, but many early Hispanic settlers of Picacho came from Manzano.

That is no doubt why the young Martín Cháves from Manzano arrived at Picacho before age eighteen with his mother, Malena.

The young Martín was already well settled there by 1870. At least the first floor of his adobe home was probably completed by then, when he was about twenty. Not long after, the second floor was added, making it the first two-story adobe house (pictured left) in the Valley.

By 1874, at age twenty-four, durable records show Martín was already an established landowner. He ultimately owned extensive property, including his Picacho farm and sheep ranch, and had many employees to herd his stock. Across the road from his home was his general store and small hotel or inn, which no longer exists, that accommodated several travelers or visitors.

According to Lincoln County lore, from a back window of that home, Don Martín shot and killed one of the fleeing Horrell brothers one day in 1873.

The lawless reputation of the Lampasas, Texas Horrell brothers preceded them when they rode, drunk, into Lincoln Town. The county sheriff ordered them to stow their weapons. That incensed the brothers. They commenced to shoot up the town and outlying Valley, killing residents. Their shooting rampage lasted several days. Finally bored with their game of cowboy-shoot-'em-up, they headed away, riding through the valley and the nearby settlement of Picacho, passing the Cháves home, where some settlers had taken refuge, as they had already begun doing for protection from Indian raids and hoodlums. From his back window, Martín shot and killed one of the brothers as they rode by. That so angered the surviving brothers that they turned back to create more mayhem.

Martín Cháves married Juana Romero, daughter of Francisco Romero, in October 1875. Their four children were born at Picacho: Modesto Cháves, who had nine children; Benjamin Cháves, who had two children; Josefita Cháves-Quintana who had four children; Maria Cháves-Baca; and the youngest, Clara Cháves, born in 1899.

All of the years he resided there, the close-knit community—comprised of multiple small valley settlements—held Don Martín Cháves in high regard. Besides farmer, sheep rancher and businessman, he was a community leader who freely dispensed legal and business advice, although he had no training in the law. He sometimes informally served as counsel for persons appearing before Justice of the Peace, George Kimbrell. Don Martín also served as Picacho postmaster for four years.

Under the Picacho heading, the booklet, <u>A History of Lincoln County Post Offices</u>, states: "Martín Cháves, in his long life, was the honored leader in important affairs. His practical advice was followed throughout the exciting era of Billy the Kid and the bloody Lincoln County War of 1877-1881. While the first postmaster was commissioned 11 June 1891, Don Martín Cháves was commissioned on 4 April 1900. He served until 15 December 1904 when his successor was appointed."

The community residents used the Cháves home for many purposes. The top floor was often converted to a chapel where Father Jose Sambrano Tafoya, known as Father Sambrano, said mass. The first floor of the house, with a large open room off the kitchen, was used as a sala for community dances.

Don Martín Cháves completed building the San Jose Church at Picacho in 1891 and deeded it to the Archdiocese of Santa Fe in 1913. Padre Sambrano, who died in 1894, might have said mass there in the last years of his life.

Phelps and Ann Anderson were married in that little San Jose Church at Picacho.

In the latter 1910s or 1920s, Don Martín Cháves moved from Picacho to Santa Fe, where he died December 8, 1931. In his latter years, he told Miguel Antonio Otero—who served nine years as Governor of the Territory of New Mexico, from 1897 to 1906, and for whom the county of Otero was named—that he believed Billy the Kid Bonney was not as bad as he was depicted in many published writings. Cháves told Otero that much of what had been written about Billy was incorrect, that the Kid had many good qualities.

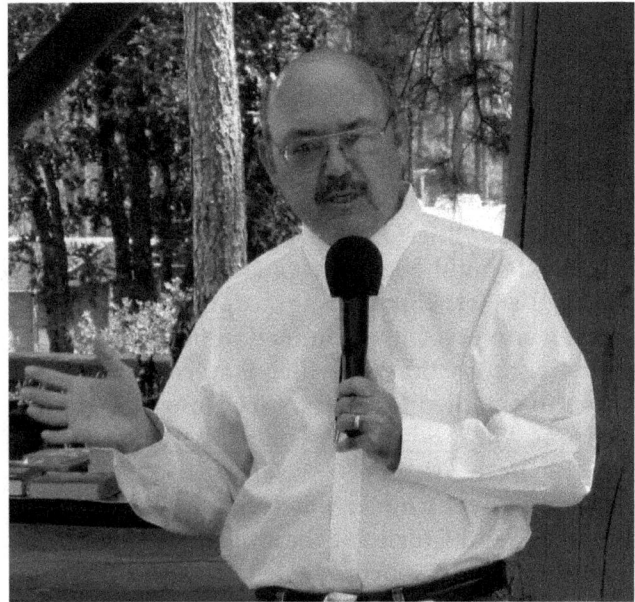

*Freddie Romero speaking to a gathering in Lincoln National Forest near Ruidoso in 2008, photo by Jan Girand*

*Freddie Romero's genealogy: Francisco Romero y Lueras and his wife Andrea Sanchez had several children, including Pablita Romero, who married Romero's great-grandfather, George Kimbrell, elected Lincoln County Sheriff in 1880, and also served as Justice of the Peace. Pablita's sister, Juanita, married Martín Cháves, who was Freddie Romero's great-great-uncle. George and Pablita Kimbrell were the parents of Freddie Romero's grandfather Juan Antonio Kimbrell, born in 1868. Father Sambrano was Romero's great-great-uncle.*

*Freddie Romero was born and grew up at Picacho, and still owns his family home there. Locally known as a person interested in Lincoln County history, Romero, an attorney, currently serves in Roswell, Chaves County, New Mexico as Judge of the Fifth Judicial District Court, Division II.*

*Phelps Anderson of Roswell, son of Robert Orville "Robert O" Anderson, and his family own Sun Valley Energy, an independent oil and gas exploration and development company. He and his family own the historic Martín Chávez home.*

# Martín Chávez addendum
## *By Jan Girand*

According to George Curry, in his *Autobiography*, published by the University of New Mexico Press in 1958, page 18 to 20: At a meeting at the Block Ranch, Billy Bonney taught him about politics. Billy predicted that George Kimbrell would beat Patrick Garrett in that voting district; Curry disagreed, but Billy was proven correct. Curry claimed in his autobiography that the officials were dishonest when they tallied the votes. (See Robert Sproull's <u>Various Authors' Accounts of Billy the Kid's Escape</u>, in this issue.)

Martín Chávez was frequently mentioned in published histories of the Lincoln County War and played an important role in the Five Day Battle in Lincoln at the height of that war.

The stage was set for the Lincoln County War prior to August 1875 by conditions caused by the L. G. Murphy, John H. Riley, Emil Fritz and J.J. Dolan group that held a business, political and power stranglehold over the county. Most of them recent Civil War military men with abundant savvy, they took advantage of the mostly uneducated pioneer settlers. In addition, many of those individuals then holding office—sheriff, county treasurer, probate clerk—were indicted for various legal infractions. Businessman Robert Casey joined the majority of those pioneer settlers in Lincoln at a political rally in an attempt to take away from them their unfair political control. But that day, William Wilson gunned down Casey, a popular man in the region, in the middle of the street on the first of August 1875. That may have been the actual beginning of the Lincoln County War.

At age twenty-four, Englishman John Henry Tunstall came to America via Canada, arrived in Santa Fe, New Mexico Territory, in late summer of 1876. There, in an establishment on San Francisco Street, he met attorney Alexander McSween of Lincoln, who talked him into going in business at Lincoln Town, which he soon did with a sizeable stake from his father in England. Together, Tunstall and McSween developed a partnership in a new mercantile business in Lincoln, in direct competition with "The House," first owned by partners Fritz and Murphy; after Fritz's departure because of poor health, their bookkeeper, Dolan, became Murphy's business partner. Friction grew to extreme animosity between the partners of the two businesses and their followers.

Tunstall hired young Billy Bonney and his pals, equipping Billy with a horse and saddle, beholding the Kid to his new English friend. In early 1878, Tunstall and a small group of hired hands, including Billy, were herding his stock of horses from his ranch through a canyon. When Tunstall became separated from his group, a posse ambushed, shot and killed him. The Lincoln County War then became a deadly armed conflict with sharply defined sides.

In April 1878, unsuspecting Sheriff William Brady and his deputy George Hindman were shot and killed in the middle of the Lincoln street near the McSween home, presumably by Billy and the Regulators. Then came the shoot-out at Blazer's Mill after the Regulators arrived there, hung out, and then opened fire on Buckshot Roberts, after he too arrived at the mill. Regulator Captain Richard Brewer and Roberts were killed and several Regulators were wounded.

Frederick Nolan wrote, on page 151 in *The West of Billy the Kid* (copyright 1998), "On Sunday evening, July 14 [1878], the Regulators came down into the Bonito Valley, where they were reinforced by a sizeable band of native New Mexicans led by Martín Chávez of Picacho. Quietly and without firing a shot, the sixty or so men occupied Lincoln, completely outnumbering and cutting off from each other the [Sheriff George] Peppin men quartered in the Wortley and the old stone Torreon, a tower built by early settlers as a defense against the Apaches." And, wrote Nolan, "Guarding McSween in his own home were the Kid and a dozen others. The rest took up strategic positions around town: Henry Brown, George Coe, and Sam Smith holed up in the adobe grain warehouse in back of the Tunstall building, Martín Chávez and perhaps twenty of his men occupied Patrón's and Montaño's, while Bowdre, Scurlock and another dozen fighting men took over the Ellis store." On page 156, Nolan wrote, "...On the opposite side and further down the street, Martín Chávez, Fernando Herrera and most of the native New

Mexicans —twenty men or more—manned the Montaño store."

For five days, the battle between the two factions continued in Lincoln Town; Col. N.A.M. Dudley of Fort Stanton, his soldiers and his howitzer trained on the McSween home, unfairly sweetened the odds in favor of "The House" and the Sheriff George Peppin faction. Susan McSween and Billy and some of his Regulators separately escaped the burning McSween home after it was torched, but Alex McSween and others were not as fortunate.

The Lincoln County War continued. Sheriff Pat Garrett shot and killed Billy in Fort Sumner on the night of July 14, 1881—exactly three years after the Five Day Battle had begun.

Even into this new millennium, descendents of Lincoln County pioneer families remain divided in their belief of which side of the Lincoln County War was right. The truth is, neither was right and all behaved as if they were above the law.

## Patrick Garrett

### By Michael E. Pitel

*Ed Cook Photo of Pat Garrett statue*

*Patrick Floyd Jarvis Garrett* (1850-1908) is at last appropriately—and publicly—honored in New Mexico. On Saturday, March 31, 2012, a larger-than-life bronze statue by Glen Rose, Texas sculptor Robert Summers was dedicated in downtown Roswell, behind the Chaves County Courthouse. It faces the 1912 *beaux artes* Neo-Classical building's east side main entrance on Virginia Avenue. There the outdoor sculpture portrays the legendary Garrett as he'd probably like to be remembered, as a larger-than-life lawman on horseback, sitting tall in the saddle, slipping a round into the chamber of his Colt revolver while searching the distances, on the hunt.

The $270,000 sculpture is Summers' second commissioned piece in Roswell and third in southeast New Mexico. His earlier Roswell bronze, a larger-than-life statue of famed local cattle baron *John Simpson Chisum* (1824-1884), mounted alongside his lead steer, a Texas longhorn named Ol' Ruidoso, is a block away. Dedicated in March 2001, the heroic $200,000 Chisum statue dominates tiny Pioneer Park, across North Main Street from the large front lawn of the green-domed courthouse.

Summers' $286,000 larger-than-life bronze statue of Chisum's niece, *Sallie Lucy Chisum Robert Stegman* (1858-1936), was unveiled in downtown Artesia in July 2003.

Leon Metz, in his acclaimed 1973 biography of Patrick Garrett, insists that Garrett's years in Uvalde, Texas—1891-1895— were his happiest. I disagree. I think Garrett's earliest years in Roswell were his happiest. He was a newlywed in 1880, when he and his bride homesteaded a 160-acre tract of land outside Roswell. A first-time father in 1881 (when daughter Ida was born), Garrett watched his family grow as son Dudley Poe and daughter Elizabeth were born in 1882 and 1885. Garrett doted on his kids, and they adored him. He became the no-nonsense, one-term Lincoln County Sheriff in 1881-82 whose campaign promise he kept. Garrett assured voters he'd bring an end to Billy the Kid's cattle rustling ways and he did just that. Less than six weeks after having been deputized shortly after his November 1880, election, he tracked down the Kid and hauled him off to the Santa Fe County Jail. When he turned over the young fugitive to Deputy U. S. Marshal Charles Conklin,

Garrett still had five days to go before being sworn in as Sheriff.

He rose to fame for having tracked down the Kid twice (the second time shooting and killing the Kid in Fort Sumner in July, 1881). Garrett chose not to run for reelection. He tried his hand at ranching and rounding up cattle rustlers again. But he wanted to do something less dangerous. He returned to his farm outside Roswell, where he grew alfalfa, harvested grapes from his vineyard, and coaxing apples and peaches from his vast orchard. Garrett expanded his farm to 1,800 acres while keeping an eye out for ways to become prosperous.

Thin-skinned to criticism and impatient with bureaucracy, he realized he would never be able to control what people thought of him for having killed the Kid. Garrett's drinking and gambling habits, which would grow in frequency and *gravitas* in the years to come, hadn't begun to take a toll on him in those early years. He hadn't begun to lean on friends and business associates for loans he didn't or couldn't repay. The bills hadn't begun to pile up yet.

In 1885, Garrett seized upon a bold idea that had the potential to transform the Pecos River Valley: Dam the deep Rio Hondo east of Roswell, just below Berrendo Creek, and move the trapped water outward into an irrigation system that would turn the semiarid landscape into lush farmland. He and wealthy Carlsbad rancher Charles B. Eddy and Santa Fe *Daily New Mexican* publisher Charles Greene agreed to form the Pecos Valley Irrigation & Investment Company. Garrett agreed to help Eddy with the promotional work. He also agreed to help Greene find additional investors back East, an effort that took three years. In September 1888, the company incorporated.

In February 1889, farmer Garrett, rancher Eddy, and local businessman Joseph C. Lea traveled to Santa Fe and successfully petitioned the Territorial Legislature to create Chaves and Eddy Counties and designate Roswell and the town of Eddy (Carlsbad) the county seats.

In 1890, Garrett became a partner in several local businesses. He and James Brent,

like Garrett a former Lincoln County Sheriff, opened a horse-drawn hack service from Roswell south through Seven Rivers and Eddy (Carlsbad) to Pecos, Texas, and back. He and Steve Mendenhall operated a Roswell livery stable. Garrett and architect J. A. Hill owned a construction company that built the fourteen-room Pauly Hotel in Roswell in 1890. Garrett also was a partner in an Eddy (Carlsbad) livery stable. He bought seven lots in the newly platted township of Eddy in 1890, as well.

Eventually the cash-strapped Pecos Valley Irrigation & Investment Company attracted the attention of an extremely wealthy Coloradoan, James J. Hagerman. By 1890, Hagerman nudged Garrett—and his five years' worth of legwork—out.

In April 1891, just months after he lost the election as Chaves County's first Sheriff by a 274-152 vote, an embarrassed, hurt, and sullen Garrett packed up Apolinaria and the children and moved to Uvalde, Texas. *Madrecita* and the kids didn't want to go. They loved Roswell.

It would be five years before Garrett returned to New Mexico for another shot at reestablishing his reputation.

But in those earliest years in Roswell, I think he felt good about himself and his chances in life. He played his fame whenever he could. His name was widely recognized. He was honest and a man of his word. I think he believed his future was in Roswell, which, like his life, was full of promise.

Garrett isn't buried in Roswell or anywhere in Chaves County for that matter.

His remains lay 150 miles west, in the well-kept Masonic Cemetery on South Compress Road in the city of Las Cruces, New Mexico. Alongside are the remains of *Apolinaria Gutierrez Garrett* (1861-1936), and seven of their eight children.

Originally Garrett had been buried in the tiny International Order of Oddfellows (IOOF) Cemetery across the street. But after the IOOF Cemetery fell victim to neglect, Garrett's youngest daughter, Pauline, had her family's remains transferred to the much larger (and better kept) Masonic Cemetery in 1957.

The earlier plot in the IOOF Cemetery is still simple and modest. It's also easy to find. It's the farthest plot from the front gate (in the closest corner to the railroad tracks outside the cemetery's east wall). There, flush against the sand is a rectangle of concrete curbing, imprinted with a single word: Garrett.

To visit the Garrett family plot in the Masonic Cemetery, drive down its middle (eastside) entrance. Just past a small utility pole on the right, look to the left for an adult mimosa tree, one of only two in the cemetery. There in its summer shade is the Garrett plot.

Today, Roswell and Chavez County have several historic sites tied to the Garretts.

Garrett's pitched-roof, six-room adobe home, where he and Apolinaria lived from 1880 until April, 1891, still stands at the north end of Bosque Road, five road miles (eight kilometers) east of downtown Roswell. The thick-walled residence was where Garrett gradually turned a quarter section of raw land into a sprawling, valuable farm.

Although it was placed on the State Register of Cultural Properties in 1986 and the National Register of Historic Places in 1988, the Garrett home, which once boasted rose bushes and bluegrass in the front yard and acquired a second story circa 1888, has languished the last couple of decades. It's currently a privately owned storage facility.

The farmhouse is also noteworthy as the place where, from August to October 1881, Garrett's longtime friend, vagabond ex-reporter and former Roswell postmaster *Marshall Ashmun Upson* (1828-94), wrote the first fifteen chapters of Garrett's 1882 book, *The Authentic Life of Billy The Kid, the Noted Desperado of the Southwest, Whose Deeds of Daring and Blood Made His Name a Terror in New Mexico, Arizona and Northern Mexico.*

It's also the place where Garrett and the alcoholic Upson operated a realty and surveyor business from March 1889 to January 1891.

The Downtown Roswell Historic District today boasts two homes with ties to the Garretts. The elegant Queen Anne-style mansion that prominent Roswell banker *John William Poe* built for his wife, Sophie, in 1895, is at 311 North Seventh Street. Poe (1851-1923) was one of Garrett's deputies outside Pete Maxwell's home in Old Fort Sumner the night that Garrett shot and killed the Kid. The Poes' place is currently undergoing renovation and restoration. Eight

blocks south of the Poes' home is the modest, five-room adobe bungalow of the Garretts' sight-impaired daughter, renowned songstress-pianist *Elizabeth Garrett* (1885-1947). Built in 1934 in the Pueblo Revival architectural style, it's hidden near the back of an extremely narrow lot at 102 South Lea Street.

Elizabeth is best remembered for having composed the song, "O Fair New Mexico," in 1915. The State Legislature adopted it as the official state song in 1916. Both homes are private residences, but can be seen from the sidewalk.

Chisum, the amiable, avuncular, and wildly successful "Cattle King of the Pecos," lived with his two younger brothers, and his niece and two nephews just five road miles (eight kilometers) southeast of downtown Roswell from December 1874 to July 1884. His vast cattle herd, grazing on belly-high, public domain grasslands for 150 miles along the Pecos River Valley, once numbered 80,000 head. Chisum's ranch, known as the Jingle Bob, was sold in 1892, eight years after his death. It remains a private residence. But motorists can see some of its homes and outbuildings from two vantage points.

The first point of view, from the east shoulder of State Road 256 (the Old Dexter Highway), is farther. It looks 500 yards (457 meters) eastward, down the stonewalled and gated main entrance, into South Springs Ranch. An extensive orchard obstructs the view in the warm-weather months. The second vantage point is 150 yards (137 meters) closer. It looks southward across the dry bed of South Spring River from the south shoulder of nearby State Road 254 (Brasher Road).

In south Roswell, some two miles (3.2 kilometers) west of Chisum's former South Springs Ranch, awaits 201-acre *South Park Cemetery, established in 1884.* Among its 29,000 graves are those of John Poe, his former deputy who'd succeeded Garrett as Lincoln County Sheriff (in 1883-84); Poe's wife, *Buckboard Days* author *Sophie Alberding Poe* (1860-1954), for whom Garrett had helped play matchmaker in 1882; rancher and business leader *Joseph Calloway Lea* (1841-1904), who'd urged Garrett in 1880 to run for the office of Lincoln County Sheriff; *Jacob Basil "Billy" Mathews* (1847-

1904), one of Lincoln County Sheriff William Brady's deputies who survived Brady's ambush killing in Lincoln on April 1, 1878 (a murder for which the Kid paid dearly); Garrett's favorite child, songbird *Elizabeth*, a Roswell resident the last 23 years of her life; and Sallie and Walter Chisum, bachelor cattle baron Chisum's niece and nephew. *Sallie Lucy Chisum Robert Stegman* (1858-1934), whom the Kid had befriended in 1878 (before her two concerned uncles and widowed father, James, had spirited her away to the safety of finishing school) lived at the Jingle Bob from 1877 to 1890, and eventually moved back to Roswell for the last 15 years of her life. Her younger brother, *Walter* (1861-1919), lived first at the Jingle Bob from 1877 to 1890, then moved into Roswell from 1890 to 1913 before moving to Oregon. Garrett's former livery stable partner, Stephen S. Mendenhall, is buried there, too. Also buried in the cemetery is *Carl Adamson* (1866-1919), an eyewitness (and possible accomplice) to Garrett's murder, six miles northeast of downtown Las Cruces, in February 1908.

Garrett's name carries instant recognition not only in New Mexico, but also throughout the U. S. His reputation was tarnished towards the end of his life, but despite his personal shortcomings, Garrett's professional reputation was a respected and feared-yet-fair law enforcement officer, tireless and unrelenting in the field endures. Like Summers' bronze statue, Garrett as Sheriff still rides tall in the saddle. In the history of Territorial New Mexico, he will always be remembered as the Lincoln County Sheriff (1881-82) who went after the young outlaw, Billy the Kid, and as the Dona Ana County Sheriff (1896-99) who pursued the men who murdered Col. Albert J. Fountain and his eight-year-old son, Henry.

It was El Paso, Texas historian Leon Metz, who, at the end of his acclaimed 1973 biography, *Pat Garrett, The Story of a Western Lawman*, had lamented that *"One can search across all of New Mexico, and indeed the entire Southwest today, and find no other monument to his memory."*

Immediately after the March 31, 2012, dedication of the Garrett statue, a beaming Metz admitted, *"included that sentence for a reason."*

*Roswell* dedicated its heroic Garrett statue at the right time in this, *the state's centennial year.* It's a fitting monument (and a fitting moment) to honor a man whose spirit embodied much of what New Mexico had aspired to be long before statehood.

## Michael Edward Pitel

*Patrick Garrett's granddaughter Susannah Garrett, Mike Pitel and his wife Pat. Photo courtesy of Bob Ross*

The eldest of four sons to an upstate New York civil engineer, Mike worked in the New Mexico state tourism office, where, from 1977 to 1999, he guided, developed, or created nearly every program in that agency, and helped it grow from a seven-person division to an 80-member department.

In 1994 Mike published a critically acclaimed *Billy The Kid Country* brochure. It was not only the first brochure ever produced about the young outlaw for state tourism industry consumption. It was also a comprehensive travel-planning tool for Billy the Kid enthusiasts and tour operators worldwide.

Shortly after taking early retirement, he was elected to the New Mexico Tourism Hall of Fame in 1999. Soon afterward, Mike founded TravelSource New Mexico, a Santa Fe-based business that creates and promotes tourism products and services for New Mexico's tourism industry, with a special emphasis on its nationally prominent historic pathways.

In 2006 Mike was hired by the state Tourism Department to direct its Billy the Kid (BTK) Project, a $200,000 initiative that understood the many historic points of interest associated with BTK, the Lincoln County War, and Pat Garrett were longtime underpublicized tourism assets. Mike inventoried dozens of historic sites on public and private land; hosted four public meetings through which he outlined a plan of action for the project; and created a Billy the Kid Web Page on the department's Web Site. The comprehensive, travel-planning Web Page included four BTK travel brochures in pdf format for travelers, tour operators, and travel media in national and international markets.

Michael Pitel, his wife—the former Patricia B. Montoya—and their son, Douglas (now a UNM student), live in Santa Fe.

## Apolinaria Gutierrez Garrett
## Wife of Patrick Garrett
### Research by Charles O. Sanders

She was born in March or April 1860, and died—at age 76-1/2 years of age—on October 21, 1936.

For durable records, primarily for census takers, Apolinaria seldom stated her age accurately. That could have been, as was often the case with census givers in that era, because in her household her birthday was unrecorded. In that era in New Mexico, even devout Catholics seldom had their own family Bibles—in which births and deaths were recorded—in their homes. In that era also, most New Mexico residents were uneducated, the females especially and, therefore, were poor at math. She probably didn't know her exact age and simply guessed. Then, unlike now,

=-=-=-=-=-=-=-=-=-=-=-=-=-=-=-=-=-

accurate birth-dates were unimportant for identification.

Sanders tracked her backwards through time, beginning with her death certificate abstract:
New Mexico Deaths, 1889-1945:
Name: Apolinoria Guturiez Garrett
Death Date: 21 Oct 1936
Death Place: New Mexico, United States
Gender: Female
Age at Death: 75
Estimated Birth Year: 1861
Spouse's Name: Patrick Garrett
Father's Name: Delores Guturiez
Mother's Name: Feliciana Valdez De Guturiez

According to census records:
In 1930, Las Cruces, she said she was 64.
In 1920 Las Cruces, she said she was 56.
In 1910 Las Cruces, she said she was 46. Her widowed mother, Feliciana Valdez de Gutierrez, age 67, lived with her in 1910. In 1900 Las Cruces, she said she was 38, born Feb 1862. Her widowed mother, Feliciana Valdez de Gutierrez, age 58, born Apr 1842, lived in Las Vegas.

In 1880 Lincoln, she said she was 20; that's a fact. Her parents, Jose Delores Gutierrez and Feliciana Valdez, lived in Fort Sumner with their six-year-old grandson, Candido. Apolinaria's sister, Celsa, age 24, lived with husband, Sabal/Saval at Cabra Arenoso.

In 1870 Puerto de Luna, it was recorded that she was 12 and Celsa was 13.

On 10 Jul 1860 in the "Town of El Tecolote," a few miles east of Las Vegas, New Mexico, she was four months old, and Celsa was two years old. That indicates Apolinaria was born in 1860, in March or April.

=-=-=-=-=-=-=-=-=-=-=-=-=-=-=-=-=-

# Did Billy the Kid Have a Kid?

## Research by Charles O. Sanders

In addition to several imaginative versions of Billy Bonney's identification and delayed death, some have now claimed to be his descendent.

Patrocino Garcia never claimed himself to be a son of William H. "Billy" Bonney. He would be amazed to learn that, in the past decade or so, his grandson has made that claim for him, and an annual play near El Paso seems to reflect that.

Abrana Segura and Martín Garcia of Fort Sumner had several children. One of those was son Patrocinio Garcia, but he was not their first-born. He had a brother, Antonio, who was more than twelve years older.

There are many durable records that attest to Patrocino's birth date, including data he himself provided. The 1900 census states Patrocinio was born March 15, 1885. In the 1910 census, he was recorded as 26; for his WWI Draft Registration Card, he said he was 33, born 15 Mar 1885; in the 1920 census listed as 34; in the 1930 census as 45. His 1964 Social Security (SSN) death record says he was born 16 Mar 1886.

It is impossible for Billy the Kid Bonney, killed on July 14, 1881, to have had a son born in 1885 or 1886.

In the below data from the Fort Sumner census, Patrocino is not yet born. But three of his siblings were. His birth/baptismal record show he wasn't born for another year.

1885 New Mexico Territorial Census
Pct. 27, Fort Sumner, San Miguel, New Mexico
Enumeration District: 23
Page: 16/A    7 Jun 1885
139/178

| Garcia, Martin | W M 39 | Husband | Herder | NM NM NM |
| Segura, Abrana | W F 27 | Wife | Keeping House | NM NM NM |
| Garcia, Antonio | W M 12 | Son | At Home | NM NM NM |
| Reveca | W F 4 | Dau | | NM NM NM |
| Rosa | W F 2 | Dau | | NM NM NM |

The household of Abrana and Martin Garcia was only a few doors from that of Abrana's brother, Alejandro. In the 1880 census, they were five doors apart; in the 1885 census, only two doors apart. In both, their parents' household was between theirs.

The woman who would eventually become Patrocinio Garcia's wife, Beatrice, was the daughter of Yginio <u>Garcia</u> and Maximiana Anaya. The death certificate of Beatrice's mother, dated 27 Mar 1936, states she was Maximiana A. Garcia, widow of Higinio Garcia, daughter of Jesus Anaya and Tomacita Baca. Many other documents confirm that genealogical information. In an additional attempt by Patrocino's grandson to rewrite history is his claim that Billy's pal, Yginio Salazar—not Yginio Garcia—was Beatrice's father. That is yet another false attempt to tie Patrocino Garcia to Billy Bonney.

Yginio Garcia, father of Beatrice, who was Patrocino's wife, was mentioned by Pat Garrett in his *The Authentic Life of Billy, The Kid*:

"*I met a Mexican named Iginio Garcia, in my rounds, whom I knew to be a tool of the Kid's, and spoke to him. I warned him not to betray my presence to any of the gang and not to leave the plaza. He represented that he had urgent business below, but assured me that he would keep my counsel. I consented that he should go, as it did not matter much. If they knew I was there, they would labor under the impression that my only support in an engagement would be Mason and, perhaps, a Mexican or two. The fact of the presence of Stewart and his party, I felt sure had not been betrayed. Garcia lived twelve miles south of Fort Sumner and [he] started in that direction.*"

Abrana Segura's older brother, Alejandro Segura, was the Justice of Peace at Fort Sumner in 1881, and served on the Coroners' Jury that found "our verdict is that the deed of said Garrett was justifiable and we are unanimous in the opinion that the gratitude of all the community is due to the said Garrett for his deed and is worthy of being rewarded."

Would the brother of Billy's lover, the uncle of Billy's future love child, applaud Billy's killer? Perhaps he would have if he knew the Kid was dallying with his married-with-children younger sister.

Far more likely, Abrana knew and liked the Kid, but was not having an illicit affair with him behind her husband's back. She would be amazed that her great-grandson now makes that claim.

=-=-=-=-=-=-=-=-=-=-=-=-=-=-=-=

Also of historical interest, a few pages/doors further in the same 1885 Fort Sumner census as that of the Garcia family, are the Maxwell families:

Page: 18/C    8 Jun 1885

163/206

| Maxwell, Luz B. | W F 58 | | Keeping House | NM NM NM |
|---|---|---|---|---|
| Odila | W F 17 | Dau | At Home | NM NM NM |
| William | W M 9 | Ward | At Home | TX TX TX |

163/207

| Maxwell, Pedro | W M 38 | Husband | Stockman | NM TX NM |
|---|---|---|---|---|
| Sara | W F 27 | Wife | Keeping House | Not known as she was not around |

And the Manuel Abreu family:

163/208

| Abreu, Manuel | W M 28 | | Stockman | NM NM NM |
|---|---|---|---|---|
| Dilia | W F 6 | | Dau | NM NM NM |

And one of the Beaubien families:

164/209

| Beaubien, Pablo | W M 38 | Husband | Stockman | NM NM NM |
|---|---|---|---|---|
| Maxwell, Reveca | W F 30 | Wife | Keeping House | NM TX NM (Rebecca Abreu) |
| Beaubien, Zenaida | W F 9 | Dau | At Home | NM NM NM |
| Maxwell, Deluvina | I F 38 | Servant | | NM NM NM |

In the above census, note that Deluvina, an Indian servant (IF=Indian, female) is in the Beaubien household, and William "Maxwell" is listed as a ward of the Luz Maxwell family. Luz was the widow of patriarch-landowner, Lucien B. Maxwell.

In the same year, 1885, in the Los Lunas, New Mexico census, is the home of Paula/Paulita Maxwell, who married Jose Jaramillo in 1883. This is the future home of Telesfor Jaramillo, who won't be born for 12 more years, in June 6, 1893. Telesfor is another who was misidentified as a love child of Billy's—also impossible.

1885 New Mexico Territorial Census
Los Lunas, Valencia, New Mexico
Enumeration District: 37
Page: 59/C    6 Jul 1885
185/191

| Jaramillo, Jose L. | W M 23 | Stockraiser | | NM NM NM |
| Paula M. | W F 20 | Wife | H.K. | NM NM NM (Paulita Maxwell) |
| Adelina | W F 1 | Dau | | NM NM NM |
| Garcia, Maria M. | W F 15 | Nurse | Nurse | NM NM NM |

/-/-/-/-/-/-/-/-/-/-/-/-/-/-/-/-/-/-/-/-/-/-/-/-/-/-/-/-/-/-/-/-/-/-/-/-/-/-/-/-/-/-/-/-/-/-/-/-/-/-/-/-/-/-/-/-/-/-/-/

## Manuel Antonio Chaves, El Leoncito
### Research by Charles O. Sanders

"Perhaps the only available photo of Manuel Antonio Chaves, used by all authors who wrote about him, this photo first appeared in Ralph Emerson Twitchell's 1909 *The History of the Military Occupation of the Territory of New Mexico from 1846 to 1851 by the Government of the United States.*" For his many feats of courage and marksmanship in multiple decisive battles, Chaves was known as El Leoncito, the Little Lion. He was born about 1818 and died in 1889. First a soldier in the Mexican Army, he later swore his allegiance to the U.S. and fought in the U.S. Civil War at the Battle of Glorieta Pass, and fought alongside Ceran St. Vrain, saving his life during the Pueblo Indians' Taos Revolt. Historian-author Marc Simmons wrote a book about one of New Mexico's earliest heroes, "the Little Lion."

## Col. Jose Francisco Chaves, for whom Chaves County was Named

### Research by Charles O. Sanders

Photo of Col. Jose Francisco Chaves
found by Charles O. Sanders in the Library of Congress collection

A bust of Col. Jose Francisco Chaves (for whom Chaves County was named) is found "at the entrance" of New Mexico's state capitol building. The caption there reads: "Col. J. Francisco Chaves was born in Los Padillas, Bernalillo County, New Mexico, June 27, 1833. Served as Lieutenant Colonel in Union Army under Kit Carson, was assassinated at 7 o'clock on the evening of Saturday, November 26, 1904 at Pinos Wells, Torrance County, New Mexico."

Excerpts from *Acts of the New Mexico Legislative Assembly*, published by the Secretary of State, 1905, page 371: "Joint Resolution 4. A Reward for the Arrest and Conviction of the Persons Who Assassinated Col. J. Francisco Chaves, and for the Accomplices in said Assassination. C. J. R. No. 4; Approved January 24, 1905. " ...on the night of November 26th, 1904, Col. J. Francisco Chaves, territorial superintendent of public instruction, and a membe- elect of the present legislative council, was most foully and cruelly assassinated by unknown parties at Pinos Wells in Torrance County, in the Territory of New Mexico; and ... it is the sense of this legislative council that the perpetrators of this outrage should be speedily discovered and punished; now therefore, ... the Council of the Thirty-sixth Legislative Assembly, the House of Representatives concurring ... the governor of this territory ... is hereby requested to offer a reward of two thousand five hundred ($2,500) dollars for the capture and conviction of the guilty parties ..."

*Photo by Jan Girand*

"Colonel José Francisco Chaves 1833-1904
Soldier—Legislator—Educator"

The above caption is on the plaque under the bust of Chaves, created by renowned sculptor Robert Summers, displayed inside the Chaves County Courthouse in Roswell, New Mexico.

The printed dedication to Colonel Chaves beside the bust reads: "José Francisco Chaves, for whom Chaves County was named when it was created in 1889, was a prominent Republican politician, former army officer in the Civil War, an avid prosecutor and legislator, and a strong advocate for [New Mexico] statehood.

Chaves was born in Las Padillas, Bernalillo County [New Mexico] on June 27, 1833. He was educated at St. Louis University and other eastern schools, where he studied the classics and medicine. As an army officer, Chaves served in the Navajo campaign in 1860. During the Civil War, he served alongside Kit Carson and Ceran St. Vrain in the New Mexico Campaign against the Confederates.

Chaves was elected Territorial delegate to Congress in 1865, where he served three terms. In the late 1870s, Chaves became a district attorney in Socorro where he was known as a strict enforcer of the law.

Chaves later served in the Territorial Legislature, and a bust of him is on display in the Capitol at Santa Fe. He was president of the council at the time Chaves County was created. Captain J.C. Lea insisted on naming the new county after Chaves instead of himself in a gesture to him for favors to the budding village of Roswell. Chaves supported Roswell's New Mexico Military Institute in its early struggles to survive. The figure at the base [inset] of the bust shows Chaves giving the New Mexico Military Institute commencement speech on May 1901 in his capacity as Territorial Superintendent of Schools.

On November 26, 1904, Chaves was having dinner with friends in Pinos Wells, Torrance County. Someone outside the house fired a shot [through a window] and killed him. The killer was never brought to justice. Many felt the political 'Santa Fe Ring' was behind the slaying.

Chaves' assassination remains one of the mysteries of New Mexico history."

# VARIOUS AUTHORS' ACCOUNTS OF BILLY THE KID'S ESCAPE
## By Robert Sproull
### Compiled more than ten years ago, from books then published.

### 1881 Background Events

| | |
|---|---|
| 9 April | Billy convicted of murdering Sheriff Brady. |
| 15 April | Judge Bristol orders Billy's execution by hanging on 13 May |
| 18 April | Deputies begin trip to Lincoln with Billy. |
| 21 April | Billy arrives in Lincoln. Confined in the Lincoln County Courthouse |
| 28 April | Billy kills Bell and Olinger; Escapes from the Courthouse. |
| 30 April | Wallace signs death warrant for Billy for Friday, 13 May |
| 14 July | Garrett shoots Billy at Fort Sumner. |

**Condensation of various author's accounts by Robert Sproull are Listed by Alphabetical Order of Authors, NOT to be Interpreted as in Order of Importance or Historical Accuracy.**

ANAYA, Paco    *I BURIED BILLY*
Creative Publishing Co, College Station, TX
1991

Paco was about Billy's age; Billy had lived with him during his last days. He didn't write his account until 1931. Paco's story is a record of what he remembers of what Billy told him about his escape, and is not in accord with any others!

Billy was handcuffed and shackled and Bell and Olinger kept at least ten feet distant from Billy at all times. On the day of his escape, Bell and Olinger took him down the inside west staircase for breakfast at a table in the sheriff's office at the foot of the stairs. The breakfast was a good one cooked by the Negro cook, Gus. (sic Gauss). When finished and starting to go upstairs, Olinger told Bell to go with Billy and he would go across the street to the bar for three cigars for the three of them. Bell followed

Billy up the stairs. Billy told Paco that he hid a knife on his person where the guards didn't discover it. When he went to the privy, he took it out and cleaned it, and used the knife to open the left side of the handcuff. When he was halfway up the stairs, he opened the cuff with the knife, which he had hidden in the fly of his pants, and when the guards got to the room where he was imprisoned, he threw the cuffs at Bell and hit him on the left temple and Bell fell. Billy took Bell's gun and shot him in the back, then grabbed Olinger's two-barrel shotgun and a Winchester rifle and ran to the window looking out to the Wortley Hotel. Olinger was beneath the window, Billy shot him and he fell dead, face up. Bell in the meantime had regained consciousness and headed for the stairs. Billy shot him with the Winchester, killing him. Billy took a belt full of 44 caliber bullets, the pistol, and the Winchester, and ordered Gus (Gauss) to bring him a horse.

Gus refused; Billy pointed the Winchester at him and he brought the horse.

**BALL, Eve** *MA'AM JONES OF THE PECOS*
Univ. of Arizona Press, Tucson, AZ      1968

The children of Lincoln ran errands for "Billicito," whom they loved. Jim Jones went to Lincoln to see Billy, but the guards would not let him in. Gauss told Jim that Billy had plans to escape and didn't want Jones to spoil them. Francisco Salazar and Florencio Chavez told Jones in Roswell how Billy did it. Olinger was at the Wortley having lunch. Billy asked Bell to take him to the outhouse. Billy had arranged to have a six-shooter wrapped in paper and left in the little building by a young boy who routinely used the outhouse. A visitor tipped Billy that the gun was in place. Billy slipped his hands out of the cuffs and on the return to the courthouse, got possession of Bell's gun. When Bell refused to open the armory and ran, Billy's shot killed him. Olinger was killed by his own shotgun when he ran back to the courthouse, and Billy called to him from an overlooking window. Gauss tossed Billy a miner's pick through the south window and Billy loosened one shackle. Gauss and Severa Gallegos, a small boy, caught a horse for Billy. The loose shackle chain spooked the horse and it took him two tries to mount it.

He took his time riding away. No effort was made to detain him.   (Pages 180 to 182)

**BARKER, Allen** *THE KID WITH FAST HANDS. A Carefully Researched History of Billy the Kid with Fictional Dialogue and Incidental Action* Self Published,
Pine Grove, CA. 1993

Billy was imprisoned in the northeast room on the second story of the courthouse.
Pat Garrett permitted Billy to have one visitor at a time, after they were searched. In Billy's room, one window faced north, the other window faced east. The line down the center of the room, over which Billy was prohibited to cross on penalty of death, allowed Billy to see out both windows. Billy's room opened into Garrett's office, which had a door to the north-south hallway and to the balcony facing the Main Street. Olinger and Bell were given the comfortable southeast apartment.

The only entrance to the second floor was a wide staircase on the southwest side of the building. The Armory was to the right of the ascending stairs. (Diagram of 2nd floor on page 386 of this reference.)

On the 28th, while Olinger had the other prisoners at the Wortley for lunch, Billy asked Bell escort him to the privy. Billy found a gun (a Colt .41 Thunderer, fully loaded) hidden by friends in the crooked ceiling vigas. He hid the gun in an old newspaper after asking Bell if he could take it back and read it. Billy went back to the courthouse, with Bell following a respectable distance behind. At the top of the stairs, Billy whirled and pointed the gun at Bell and warned him not to move. Bell broke for the stairs and Billy's shot killed him.

Olinger was killed when he raced back to the courthouse and Billy emptied Olinger's own shotgun into him. (The author includes the conversation preceding the shooting as going: Gauss: "Hey Bob, the Kid just killed Bell!" Billy: "Hello, Bob."  Olinger: "Me, too.") Gauss threw Billy a prospector's pick and Billy managed to break the leg shackle chain. Gauss brought him Billy Burt's horse and Billy finally got seated in the saddle. He spoke to his admirers, then left armed with a 44-40 Colt Peacemaker and a 73 Winchester rifle of the same caliber.

**BRANCH, Louis Leon** *LOS BILLITOS. BILLY THE KID AND HIS GANG*  Carlton Press, Inc.,
New York, NY   1980

(Author claims this book was primarily based on a handwritten manuscript from 1880 by Charles Frederick Rudulph, a member of the posse that captured Billy.)

Billy was confined in the northeast room. Bell and Olinger had the southeast apartment. Bell and Billy played cards constantly while Billy waited for the May 13 execution date, and Bell grew careless. With Pat in White Oaks and Olinger at the Wortley getting lunch for the prisoners, Billy struck! While they played cards, Billy's hands were removed from the handcuffs. The cuffs weighed three pounds and Billy picked up and stunned Bell with a blow to the side of his head. When Bell ran for the stairs, Billy shot and killed him with his own gun. Olinger heard the shot and raced to the Courthouse. Olinger was killed with his own shotgun as Billy called to him, "Hello, Bob," and he looked up. Billy picked up a Winchester, two six-shooters and ammunition, and ordered Gauss to saddle him a horse.

Many people from the village wished him well as he rode off.

(GAUSS'S ACCOUNT of the escape as recorded in the January 15th, 1890, Lincoln County Leader is the next subject in this book by Branch. It is already mentioned in other places in this review and won't be repeated here, but some researchers may want it as an available reference. Pages 241 to 243)

From Lincoln Billy rode west toward Fort Stanton, then north through Baca Canyon toward the ranch of his friend Juan Padillo. He left the horse and took off on foot up the canyon to Jose Cordova's house a few miles west of Padillo's. Cordova and his son Manuel helped Billy remove the heavy shackles. Billy wouldn't stay but pushed on to Ygenio's home. Late that night, he staggered into Las Tablas at the base of the Capitans.

BREIHAN, Carl W.    *BILLY THE KID. A DATE WITH DESTINY* with BALLERT, Marion Superior Publishing Co., Seattle WA .  1970

On the 27th of April, Garrett left for Las Tablas to collect taxes and to White Oaks to get a scaffold built. Sam Corbett alerted Billy that a pistol was hidden in the latrine for him. On the 28th, Billy waited until Olinger took the prisoners to the Wortley Hotel for dinner. Billy asked to be taken to the latrine and found the pistol that Sam Corbett's note told him that Jose M. Aguayo had hidden. He exited the latrine and when within three or four feet of Bell, jerked out the gun and told Bell to walk through the rear door and up the stairs. When Bell reached the top, he suddenly turned and bolted for the stairs. Billy's ricochet shot killed Bell as he ran out the rear entrance and died in Gauss's arms. Billy hobbled quickly to his own cell room and the east window. Billy shouted, "Hello, Bob" as he fired Olinger's shotgun into him and killed him. He then went out on the balcony and hurled the gun at Bob saying, "Take this also!" He gathered several

Winchesters and Colt revolvers and ammunition from the Armory and ordered Gauss to throw him a pick and saddle him a horse. (George Coe was said to be aware of the latrine pistol story but withheld the information in *Frontier Fighter* to protect then-living participants.  Numerous other historians are identified as subscribing to the pistol in the latrine version. It is pointed out that Bell's pistol was found in its holster and unfired.) (Page 107 to 116)

BRENT, William    *THE COMPLETE AND FACTUAL LIFE OF BILLY THE KID* New York NY    1964

Olinger tried to terrorize Billy. Bell was more tolerant and played cards with Billy and let him slip his handcuffs off so he could handle the cards easier. He also allowed him to meander around his little room and look out the windows. It is evident now that Billy was casing his surroundings and memorizing the town's activities and the location of all the features inside and outside of the Courthouse. The twice-daily trips to the outside privy were also used to familiarize him with his surroundings, and were never made when Olinger was present.

On the fateful April 28th, Garrett was in White Oaks, Olinger was at the Wortley getting the prisoners fed, and Billy asked Bell to take him to the privy. On the return to the Courthouse, Billy got ahead of Bell coming up the stairs, went out of sight at the landing, burst open the flimsy Armory door, grabbed a loaded six shooter, whirled back to the head of the stairs and killed Bell with a ricochet shot. Billy looked out the south window and saw Bell fall, grabbed Olinger's shotgun, hurried to his east window and waited for Olinger. Geiss told Olinger that the Kid had killed Bell and when Billy said, "Hello Bob, old compadre," Olinger realized his time had come and said, " Yes, and he's killed me too!"  The buckshot was pea size, killing Olinger immediately, but Billy sent the second barrel into the dead body, broke the shotgun and hurled that at the body also. Geiss brought Billy a file and the chain between Billy's legs was separated. Geiss then saddled Billy Burt's horse. On the second try, Billy managed to stay on the horse and rode out of Lincoln to the west with a flourish of arms.

Other Escape theories on pages 180 and 181:

1. Friend concealed a gun in the privy.
2. Kid slipped out of handcuffs, got Bell's gun.
 According to author Brent, both stories probably false.    (Pages 173 to 184)

BROTHERS, Mary Hudson    *BILLY THE KID*
Hustler Press    Farmington, NM    1949

With Pat Garrett gone on the 28th of April, Billy decided to make his move for freedom. Olinger took the prisoners to the Wortley for lunch and Billy told Bell he had to go to the toilet. Bell locked the guardhouse door, leaving the key in the lock and they went down the stairs and Billy went to the privy. On the return trip Billy raced ahead up the stairs, ignoring Bell's command to stop. At the top of the stairs, Billy broke into the armory by throwing his weight against the flimsy door and lock, grabbed a pistol and in an exchange of fire with Bell, killed Bell. Olinger heard the shot, raced over and expected the Kid to appear around the corner of the Courthouse, but instead Billy called to him from the east window of his cell, " Hello, Bob!" and gave him both barrels of Olinger's own shotgun, then broke the gun and hurled the pieces at him. After killing Bell and Olinger, Billy removed the handcuffs. A rivet was driven out of the leg shackles and the chains were attached to his cartridge belt.  (Pages 43, 48)

BURNS, Walter Noble    *THE SAGA OF BILLY THE KID*    Doubleday, Page & CO.
 New York NY    1926

Billy and Bell were playing a game of Monte and Olinger had taken the prisoners to lunch. Billy kept maneuvering closer to Bell across the table. Billy "accidentally" knocked a card to the floor; when Bell bent to retrieve it, Billy snatched Bell's pistol from Bell's waistband where he carried it that day. When Bell stood up, he was looking into the barrel of his own gun. When Bell attempted to flee, Billy shot and killed him.
Grabbing Olinger's shotgun, Billy killed Olinger, after saying, "Hello, Bob!" with a shot from the east window. He then went out on the balcony and unleashed another shot into the lifeless body, broke the shotgun over the rail and hurled it down at Olinger's body. Billy took a

Winchester rifle and two six-shooters from the armory, loaded them with cartridges and then loaded the loops of one cartridge belt with pistol ammunition and the other with Winchester bullets. (The six-shooters and the Winchester actually used the same ammunition.) Goss (Gauss) cut the shackle chain between Billy's legs and brought Billy Burt's pony. After several tries Billy got mounted and waved farewell to the men and left at an easy gallop whistling a tune.
 Billy rode west out of Lincoln. (Pages 241 to 263)

COE, George W.    *FRONTIER FIGHTER*
Houghton-Mifflin Co.   New York NY    1934

After sentencing, Billy was jailed on the second floor of the old Murphy building, handcuffed and shackled and guarded constantly by his two worst enemies, Bell and Olinger. Billy stayed cheerful, always looking for that one chance in a million to get free. Bell gradually got friendly with Billy (perhaps in part because of Olinger's cruelty) and he and Billy played cards, over Olinger's objections to Garrett. While Olinger was at the Wortley feeding the prisoners, Bell and Billy played cards. When Bell leaned over to pick a card off the floor, Billy saw his chance and grabbed Bell's pistol. Bell was killed when he attempted to escape down the stairs. Olinger was killed by his own shotgun when he raced back from the Wortley at the sound of gunfire. Billy shot him from the east window after calling down, "Hello, Bob." Billy forced the jailer to chop the shackle chain and after several tries mounted a horse brought to him. (It has been written that Coe knew the true story of Billy's escape—the hidden pistol—but would not divulge it in order to protect some who were then still living.) (Pages 152, 153)

CUNNINGHAM, Eugene. *TRIGGERNOMETRY*
Press of the Pioneers, Inc.  New York NY 1934

When Olinger took the prisoners to the Wortley Hotel at noon, Billy asked Bell to take him to the latrine; on return Billy raced up the stairs and broke into the armory, snatched up a six-shooter and ran to the stairs and shot Bell with a ricochet shot, killing him. He then ran to the window and killed Olinger with his own shotgun as he raced to the courthouse.

Cunningham reports the conversation before the shooting: Geiss: "Bob, the Kid has just killed Bell!" Kid: "Hello!" Olinger: "Yes, and he has killed me, too!" Geiss threw a file to Billy and went to procure a horse. Billy stayed on the second floor for about an hour. He was like a maniac or a drunken man. He sang, he danced, he whistled, he yelled.

At last he mounted the horse Geiss brought him after he was able to file the chain apart. He had a Winchester and two revolvers, and rode out of Lincoln. Billy lived at cow camps, sheep camps and friends' adobe houses around Fort Sumner. He'd escaped from Lincoln on 28 April 1881 and was killed on 14 July 1881. (Page 163, 164)

CURRY, George    AN AUTOBIOGRAPHY
Univ. of New Mexico Press, Albuquerque, NM 1958

After the Kid was sentenced to hang on 13 May, he was taken to Lincoln to be imprisoned on the second floor of the Lincoln County Courthouse, which Garrett used as a jail. The Kid was imprisoned in what was called the guardroom, adjoining the Sheriff's office on the 2nd floor. Curry's theory of Billy's escape is that Billy slipped his hand out of the handcuff as he and Bell ascended the stairs on the way back from the outhouse. Billy then whirled around, grabbed Bell's pistol and shot him. After killing Bell, he ran to the east window and shot and killed Olinger with his own shotgun as he raced back from the Wortley. Curry reports the conversation before Olinger's death as follows: Geiss: "The kid just killed Bell." Billy: "Hello, old boy." Olinger: "Yes, and he's just killed me too."

The Kid loosened one leg shackle with a file furnished by Gauss and rode away on Billy Burt's horse that Gauss had procured for him. He went up the Rio Bonito and up Baca Canyon and through a gap in the Capitan Mountains to Las Tablas. There he stopped at Eugenio Salazar's home and sent Billy Burt's horse back with a boy. Billy remained at Las Tablas for two days. Stole Andy Richardson's horse (on the Block Ranch) and rode to Fort Sumner. (Page 42, 43)

FULTON, Maurice G.    HISTORY OF THE LINCOLN COUNTY WAR
University of Arizona Press, Tucson AZ 1968

(Robert Mullin completed this book after Fulton's death in 1955.)

Six days after being jailed with handcuffs and leg irons in the Lincoln County Courthouse (old Dolan store), Billy killed Bell and Olinger and escaped.

How did he get the pistol?

Theory # 1: Slipped hands out of the cuffs during a card game and grabbed Bell's pistol. (Bell's pistol was still in its holster at the inquest.)

Theory # 2: Bell takes Billy to the privy outside the Courthouse. Coming back, Billy raced up the stairs and got a pistol from the armory. Shot Bell.

Theory # 3: Pistol hidden in the privy by Jose M. Aguayo. (Lincolnites had use of the Courthouse privy.) Sam Corbett slipped Billy a note with "privy" on it after the pistol was placed. Billy found the pistol and when they returned to the second floor, he pulled the pistol on Bell. Bell ran and Billy shot him.

(Fulton stated that today [1955] Garrett's account, Theory # 2, is the official explanation.)

After Bell fell dead in the courtyard behind the Courthouse, there is little divergence in the accounts. The Kid then hopped to the east window, called to Olinger as he passed beneath the window, and killed Olinger with his own loaded shotgun. With a pick that Gauss tossed him, Billy removed one leg shackle so he could mount a horse.

Billy shook hands with the Lincolnites and left on Billy Burt's pony. (Pages 392 to 397)

GARRETT, Pat F.    THE AUTHENIC LIFE OF BILLY THE KID  New Mexican Printing and Publishing Co.  Santa Fe NM    1882

NOLAN, Frederick   An ANNOTATED EDITION (Of the above book) University of Oklahoma Press, Norman OK  2000

Olinger took the other prisoners to the Wortley for supper, leaving Bell in charge. Bell accompanied Billy to the outside privy of the Courthouse. Billy got considerably ahead of Bell on the return, bounded noiselessly up the stairs after turning the bend, shouldered his way into the armory, seized a six-shooter and was waiting for Bell when he reached the landing twelve steps below Billy. When Bell ran, Billy shot and watched from the south window as Bell fell dead out in the corral behind the Courthouse. Billy slipped out of the handcuffs and threw them at Bell. He then grabbed Olinger's shotgun out of Garrett's office and shot Olinger from the east window of the room Billy had been held in and Olinger fell dead. Billy then went through Garrett's office to the balcony and emptied the second barrel into Olinger. The next stop was the armory where he took a Winchester rifle and two revolvers. With a file Geiss threw to him, Billy managed to free the shackles from one leg. Geiss was ordered to bring Billy the horse that belonged to Billy Burt, Deputy Clerk of Probate.

Billy rode out of Lincoln on Billy Burt's horse with the shackles still attached to one leg and went west towards Fort Stanton. Turned north after four miles toward Las Tablas.

Garrett had been in Las Tablas on 27 April collecting taxes. On the 29th he got a report from John Delaney, Esq. of Fort Stanton that Billy killed his guards and escaped. Garrett returned to Lincoln on the 30th and tried to find the Kid's trail but failed. Billy Burt's horse came in dragging a rope. The next report said that Billy had been at Las Tablas and had stolen a horse from Andy Richardson. Pages 120 - 122)

Nolan's Comments for this portion of Garrett's Book:

"Geiss" was actually Gottfried Georg Gauss (1853-1902), a German priest who had served in the U. S. Army for ten years and came to Lincoln in the 1870's. Was cook and handyman for Tunstall; odd job man in Lincoln. Nolan thinks it highly improbable that Billy could have moved noiselessly up the staircase since he wore leg irons. More likely Billy struck Bell over the head with the handcuffs or someone left a gun in the toilet for Billy. Gauss said he threw a miner's pick to Billy during the escape, not a file.

Montgomery Bell was a black freedman, and in later years a prominent citizen of Las Vegas. (Pages 165-170)

HUNT, Frazier    *THE TRAGIC DAYS OF BILLY THE KID*  Hastings House Publishers, New York NY    1956
    (Good map of Lincoln County on the inside hard covers)

Hunt thinks the sequence of events leading to Billy's escape as determined by Fulton before his death in 1955 is as near the truth as can be determined.

The day before the escape, Sam Corbett slipped Billy a note saying Jose Aguayo had hidden a pistol in the vigas of the privy. When Bell and Billy returned from the privy, Billy threw down on Bell from several feet away and forced him to return to the second floor of the Courthouse. Bell attempted to run back down the stairs and Billy killed him with a ricochet shot. Billy shot Olinger from the east window with Olinger's shotgun after calling down to him, "Hello Bob." He then went out on the balcony and gave him the other barrel. Billy warned the natives not to come near and with Gauss's help removed one shackle and got Billy Burt's horse.

An hour or so after the shootings, Billy rode west toward Fort Stanton. He turned north on the first trail that wound its way through a gap in the Capitans and stopped at Jose Cordova's home in the foothills of the Capitans as twilight approached. Cordova and a neighbor, Sepio Salazar, removed the leg irons. Billy continued to Ygenio Salazar's home in Las Tablas as it was growing dark. Ygenio helped Billy steal a prize horse named Don from the Block Ranch. Billy knew all the water holes and started for Fort Sumner, about 100 miles away. (Pages 278 to 316)

JACOBSON, Joel   *SUCH MEN AS BILLY THE KID*   University of Nebraska Press, Lincoln, Nebraska    1994
    Theories of escape:
        Garrett - Billy bounded up the stairs on the return from the privy, broke into the Armory and shot Bell.
        Utley - The Kid slugged Bell with his handcuffs and wrestled the gun from him.
        Corbett - Someone left a key or lock pick in the outhouse for Billy.
        Corbett - Someone left a pistol in the outhouse for Billy.

Garrett gives the only explanation for how the Kid managed to free his hands from the manacles: he "slipped the handcuffs over his hands." (Author wonders: Why would Garrett and his men put oversized cuffs on their most heavily guarded prisoner? They would have seen they were loose.) It took Billy about an hour after the shooting of Bell and Olinger to leave Lincoln. Others on Billy's side restrained two citizens who were about to interfere. With the miner's pick furnished by Gauss, Billy got rid of one leg shackle and mounted the horse Gauss had caught for him.

Billy rode out of Lincoln on Billy Burt's horse. (Pages 230 to 233)

KADLEC, Robert F. *THEY "KNEW" BILLY THE KID (INTERVIEWS WITH OLD-TIME NEW MEXICANS)* Ancient City Press, Santa Fe NM 1987

These stories were gathered under the auspices of the Federal Writers Project during the Great Depression. The WPA guides were tied to this program. Obviously some of those interviewed were only repeating tales they had heard, others actually knew Billy—some with accurate memories, some with memories distorted by time.

Attributed To PAP JONES
Collected by Katherine Ragsdale
(Pap was the husband of Ma'am Jones) When Billy was in or near Lincoln, Bob Olinger killed John Jones, (Pap's son) in Pierce Canyon by what many called cold-blooded murder. Pap Jones went to Lincoln to settle the debt. When Pap met Billy in a saloon and told him he was there to settle it with Olinger, Billy told him he was too old to do that and was needed back home. If he went home, Billy promised he would take care of it. Pop got the word after Billy escaped that the debt had been paid. (Pages 57, 58)

PACO ANAYA of Vaughn
Collected by Edith L Crawford
Paco said a writer claimed Billy rode sideways (side-saddle) for twenty miles after his escape because he was still burdened with the leg-irons and chain. This was not true because Goss had separated the chain with an ax on the wood block outside the cooking cabin. Goss said he had threatened Olinger because of insults Olinger made about his cooking to Garrett. He hated Olinger and liked Billy so had no compunction about helping him. Billy rode out of town on a horse that Goss got for him—waving his hat. Billy went straight to a plaza twenty miles around the mountain and got an old Mexican ranchman to remove the leg irons with his blacksmithing outfit. The Kid changed mounts at Fort Sumner and went to Arroya Cibola, twelve miles below Fort Sumner to the ranch of old man Anaya where Paco lived. (Pages 58 -60)

LADISLADO SALAS of Lincoln
Collected by Edith L. Crawford
Salas was seven or eight years old when Billy escaped. He had gone with his father to visit Billy at the Courthouse about three times. Billy stopped at their house after the escape and had two six-shooters strapped across his shoulders and a rifle in his hand—and was riding sideways on a black horse. Salas went out into the fields and got his father and Billy stayed and ate with them. His father helped get the shackles off. Billy had his handcuffs in his pocket. The Kid was a short man and had a black mustache. (Page 61)

SAM FARMER of Carrizozo
Collected by Edith L. Crawford
The Farmer family all liked Billy. The day that he killed Bell and Olinger, he stopped where he (Sam) and his father were irrigating the fields and told them what happened. He rode off as fast as he could go and Sam could see the shackles on his legs. He was riding straddle. Billy was straight and slender, light brown hair and green eyes. His cowboy hat had a straight brim in front and was turned up in the back. The light colored hat was always on the side of his head. When he ate, he sat with his legs straight out in front of him with his plate in his lap and his hat on his boots. "That's a quick way to get up if I have to." (Pages 61 to 63)

KELEHER, William *VIOLENCE IN LINCOLN COUNTY* University of New Mexico Press, Albuquerque NM 1957

The Kid killed Bell and Olinger and left Lincoln without opposition. Garrett was in

White Oaks at the time, some say to have a gallows built with lumber from Las Tablas, "The Boards." ( Full GAUSS account on Pages 337 to 339 )

Billy rode east (?) down the road on Billy Burt's mare until he reached the home of Higinio Salazar, a trusted friend .The leg irons were removed and Billy struck out toward the Pecos River and Fort Sumner.   (Pages 332 to 346)

METZ, Leon C.   *PAT GARRETT, THE STORY OF A WESTERN LAWMAN*   University of Oklahoma Press   Norman OK  1974

A large posse accompanied Billy from Mesilla to Lincoln for three reasons:
1 .   Prevent Billy from breaking free.
2 .   To guard against a rescue attempt.
3 .   To guard against assassination.

When Olinger took the other prisoners to the Wortley Hotel at noon on 28 April, Billy asked Bell to take him to the outside toilet. Billy found the pistol left in the toilet by confederates and hid it in his shirt. On the return, Billy bounded up the stairs, whirled and told Bell to surrender—or struck him over the head with the handcuffs—"depending upon which account one prefers to accept." Bell turned and reeled down the stairs. Billy fired twice and a ricochet bullet entered Bell's body and killed him. The Kid then hobbled across the floor to Olinger's loaded shotgun and went to the east window of the room in which he had been chained. Gauss called to Olinger, "The Kid has killed Bell!" A popular story, doubted by many, is that Olinger said, "Yes, and he's killed me too!" The shotgun blast killed Olinger instantly. Billy fired the second barrel at Olinger from the balcony, broke the gun on the railing and hurled the pieces at the body with a curse. Gauss gave Billy a small prospector's pick and Billy was able to remove one shackle.

After an hour, he fastened the loose shackle to his belt and went out for the horse that had been brought to him. Despite the time it had taken, Billy paused long enough to shake hands with some of the citizens. He then galloped away. (Pages 91 to 94)

MORGAN, Leon   *BILLY THE KID*
Whitman Publishing Co., Racine, Wisc.   1935

After Olinger took the prisoners to lunch (LaRue is in this version), Billy asked Bell to take him downstairs to the old Murphy store so he could see what it was like. Bell reluctantly agreed. Billy pretended that it was hard to walk with the leg irons and stumbled down the stairs. At the bottom of the stairs, Bell's eyes wavered for a second and Billy said, "Look out, Bell!" and pointed over his shoulder. When Bell looked, Billy sprang up the stairs. Bell wheeled and threw his rifle to his shoulder. He sprang up the stairs into the barrel of a rifle Billy had seized from the armory. Bell pretended to drop his pistol, but leaped forward. Billy fired.

Billy then ran to the window overlooking the street in time to see Olinger racing to the courthouse. Billy called, "Oh, Olinger, remember what I told you?" Olinger looked up and Billy fired. No one was brave enough to challenge Billy. He used soap to lather his hands and wrists and slip off the cuffs. He made an old man saw the leg irons, tied the chain to his waist, picked a horse, and rode out of town.

NOLAN, Frederick   *THE LINCOLN COUNTY WAR*   University of Oklahoma Press, Norman, OK   1992

Olinger took the prisoners (other than Billy) across the street to the Wortley Hotel at noon on the 28th of April, leaving Bell to guard Billy. Gauss said he heard a shot as he crossed the yard behind the Courthouse and Bell ran out the door and died in his arms. He raced to the garden gate to escape and saw Olinger coming and shouted that Billy had killed Bell. Billy called out to Olinger from the window above him and Olinger fell dead from a shotgun blast. When Gauss started to run for safety, Billy called to him that he wouldn't hurt him and to get Judge Leonard's horse. Gauss threw Billy a prospecting pick to remove the leg shackles and after an hour Billy got one shackle free. Billy tied the shackle chain to his waist-belt and came out to where Gauss had saddled Billy Burt's small skittish pony, the only one available. When Billy passed Bell he said he was sorry; when he passed Olinger, he gave him a tip with his boot.

Billy shook hands all around and, after being thrown once, mounted the pony and rode off rejoicing. "He stopped at Ygenio Salazar's house west of town where his young friend helped him get the shackles off his feet and "rustle up" - the exact verb used—a good horse. Ygenio brought him a prize bay named Don that belonged to Andy Richardson and the Kid mounted up and moved out." (A quote from Utley's "The Tragic Days of Billy the Kid." Page 420 of Nolan's book.)

Nolan points out flaws in Gauss's account but explains some of them. Recounts the story that Jose Aguayo placed the pistol in the outhouse. Billy left well armed. Garrett concluded that the whole town was terror-struck. (Pages 417 to 420)

NOLAN, Frederick    *THE WEST OF BILLY THE KID*    University of Oklahoma Press, Norman, OK    1998

At the usual time on the 28th Olinger took the prisoners to lunch at the Wortley. Bell and the Kid remained in the Courthouse. Gauss was working outside. Endless theories have been advanced about what happened next. Somehow, in a series of swift and decisive moves, Billy got hold of a pistol and shot and mortally wounded Bell. Gauss heard a shot and then a tussle and Bell ran out of the stair area and died in Gauss's arms. The most plausible theory is that there was a pistol hidden in the outside privy for Billy. However Bell was killed, Billy proceeded to the next phase and emptied Olinger's shotgun into him when he raced over from the Wortley at the sound of gunfire. Billy was waiting with "Hello, Bob!" and a load of buckshot. Billy collected a Winchester and two six-shooters from Garrett's gun store and addressed the crowd from the balcony. With a prospector's pick furnished by Gauss, Billy slowly removed one leg shackle then went down and mounted Billy Burt's pony that Gauss had corralled and left—according to some—singing.   (Page 226)

OTERO, Miguel Antonio  *THE REAL BILLY THE KID*  Rufus Rockwell Wilson, Inc., New York NY   1936

Otero gives several accounts of Billy's escape. In one version he quotes Martín Chaves, whom he saw in Santa Fe after a visit to Fort Sumner in the 1930's, to settle the authenticity of the Kid's

death. Chaves had been an active participant in the Lincoln County War. The following is a condensation of Otero's quotes of Chaves' remarks, but not the exact quotes.

"Most accounts of the Lincoln County War are far from true. The account of the killing of the Kid, published by E. A. Brininstool, is correct. It was written by John W. Poe." About eighteen days before Billy's scheduled hanging, Otero, Sam Corbett, Capt. Baca and his wife visited Billy. Olinger would not let Baca in, saying he had been too friendly with Billy. A line had been drawn on the floor in the room where the Kid was held and the Kid was told not to cross it on penalty of death. While Olinger and the prisoners were at the Wortley for lunch, Billy stepped a foot across the line and was severely reprimanded by Bell. As Bell approached, Billy slowly retreated, then stopped and half turned as though to listen. Catching Bell off guard he jerked Bell's gun from its holster and ordered Bell to go into a room. Bell attempted to run down the stairs and Billy shot and killed him. Olinger heard the shot, rushed over and was shot by Billy after calling down to him, 'Hello, Bob. Please turn around so I can look you in the face.' Billy then went out on the overlooking balcony, fired a second shot into Olinger's dead body, and broke the shotgun and threw the pieces at Olinger and said, 'Take that, too, damn you .You won't follow me anymore with that gun.' Billy hobbled down the back stairs and had Gauss cut the chain with an ax and told Gauss to bring him Billy Burt's horse. To keep the people away, he stuck a rifle near his hat on a board and aimed the rifle toward the street to make them think he was ready to shoot. Everyone was happy to see the Kid escape and no one did anything to prevent it. J. A. LaRue, proprietor of the saloon, grabbed a shotgun but his wife convinced him to not interfere. Billy gave a short speech, mounted Billy Burt's horse and left singing:

I go to the plains with such sadness
And never shall I return.
And with patience I'll wait for my passing,
And no one will weep when I'm gone.

According to Chaves, Billy Burt's horse returned to Lincoln about two hours later with a thank-you note from Billy.    (Pages 160 to 173)

POE, John W. *THE DEATH OF BILLY THE KID* Houghton, Mifflin Co. Boston, MA 1933

When Pat Garrett received the Order of Execution from Governor Wallace, he wrote on the Order: "I certify that I rec'd the within named William Bonney, alias Kid, alias William Antrim, into my custody on the 21st day of April AD 1881. And further certify that on April 28th the said William Antrim made his escape by killing his guards, J. W. Bell and Robert Olinger in Lincoln, Lincoln Co., New Mexico." (Page XXXIII)

SIMMONS, Marc *WHEN SIX-GUNS RULED* Ancient City Press, Santa Fe NM 1990

(Agrees with Adams that Billy only killed six, with possibly three others.) His celebrated escape on April 28, 1881, caused the death of Bell and Olinger. A question left for historians is: How did the Kid obtain the gun used to escape? Now it is believed that a friend hid a six-shooter in the outdoor privy. Pat was in White Oaks to purchase lumber for Billy's gallows. Olinger is generally accepted as a bully and murderer. Susan McSween said, "Billy was not half as bad as his enemies, who were determined to kill him. He was neither a bad man nor a murderer, and did not kill wantonly; most of those he shot richly deserved it." Years after Governor Otero met Billy, it was his opinion that "Billy the Kid sinned less than he was sinned against." (Pages 60 to 64)

SIRINGO, Chas. A. *A TEXAS COWBOY* or *FIFTEEN YEARS ON THE HURRICANE DECK OF A SPANISH PONY* M. Umbdenstock & Co., Chicago Illinois 1885

Pat had to go to White Oaks on the 28th of April and admonished the guards to be extra vigilant. There were five other prisoners, but they were in jail for their own safety after killing four Mexican ranchers in a water rights dispute. When Olinger took these prisoners, who were permitted to wear their guns, to the Wortley for their meal, Billy was left alone with Bell. (Siringo said he received his information about Billy's escape from Chas. Wall, one of the five prisoners.) When Bell became engrossed in a

newspaper, Billy slipped one of his hands out of the handcuffs and struck Bell a stunning blow to the head. When Bell ran to the stairway for safety, Billy shot and killed him with his own gun. Billy then hobbled to where Olinger's loaded shotgun sat. When Olinger raced over from the restaurant, Billy called down to him and killed him with a shotgun blast from the east window. Billy went out on the balcony and shot him again, then broke the gun on the railing and hurled the pieces at the body, saying, "Take that, you son of a bitch! You will never follow me with that gun again!" All of this was witnessed by nearly one hundred bystanders, most sympathized with the Kid. "His enemies hunted their holes and tried to pull the hole in after them." Billy took a good Winchester rifle and two Colt 45 pistols and four belts of cartridges from the armory. A file was thrown up to him and he ordered the Deputy County Clerk's pony be brought to him, "double quick!"

The shackles were separated and after two tries, Billy mounted the pony, bid everyone adieu, and joyfully rode out of town to the west. After traveling about four miles, he turned northeast, across the Capitan Mountains, toward Fort Sumner. (Pages 275 to 280)

SONNISCHSEN, C. L. *ALIAS BILLY THE KID* University of N. M. Press, Albuquerque NM 1955

(This is the book Sonnischsen wrote with William Morrison about Brushy Bill Roberts, *a fictional character.*)

On a visit to the Lincoln County Courthouse with Morrison, "Billy" talked about his escape. At the time of the escape, there were no outside stairs to the second floor. The stairway began on the first floor on the west side and ran east. In the room where Billy was confined, Olinger taunted Billy the morning of the breakout as he loaded his shotgun in Garrett's office. Billy considered Bell a nice man. The day before the escape, Sam Corbett and his wife passed Billy a note that Sam had hidden a pistol in the latrine, but as it turned out, he didn't need it. When Olinger went to lunch, Billy asked Bell to unlock the chain and take him to the latrine. Bell first said "No," then got up and turned to get the key in Garrett's office. Billy slipped his right hand out of the cuff and swung it at Bell with his left hand, hitting him in the back of the head. Bell got up looking into the barrel of his own pistol. When Billy told Bell to take him to the armory, Bell made a break for the stairs and Billy's shot killed him. Billy's killing of Olinger was "The happiest moment of my life!" Gauss cut the chain between Billy's legs. From the armory Billy took a belt of 44 Winchester ammunition, a 44 Winchester rifle, and two single-action Colt pistols.

He rode west out of town and up a canyon where his shackles were removed. He rode over the Capitans to Higenio Salazar's home where he was fed. (Page 40 to 48)

TURNER, George E.  *SECRETS OF BILLY THE KID*  Baxter Lane Company, Amarillo, TX 1974

Billy was held in the Lincoln County Courthouse to await his execution. He was chained and shackled and directed to remain in the east half of the room in the northeast corner on the second floor. Thousands of words have been written describing the details of the Kid's escape but these must all be considered with skepticism. Nobody really knows what happened inside the building, such as how Billy got the gun. Gauss's account is the closest to an eyewitness telling of events, but there is suspicion that he didn't tell all he knew. According to Gauss, Bell fell dead at his feet after Billy shot him, and Olinger was killed by a shot from an overlooking window. Billy got rid of one leg shackle with a pick Gauss threw to him.

He rode out of town on the horse Gauss had brought to him—after shaking hands with the natives who were watching. Billy told Pete Maxwell that Bell fired at him twice. (Author's note: Probably not true.)     (Page 57)

UTLEY, Robert M.    *BILLY THE KID A SHORT AND VIOLENT LIFE*   Univ. of Nebraska Press, Lincoln, Nebraska 1989

When Olinger took the prisoners to eat at the Wortley at 6: 00 p.m., Billy asked Bell to take him to the latrine. On the return, Bell carelessly lagged behind. Billy reached the top of the stairs before Bell, slipped the cuffs off one wrist and swung the loose cuff in vicious blows that laid out two gashes on Bell's scalp. Bell went down and Billy got Bell's pistol and shot him. Bell tumbled down the stairs, raced out into the corral and fell dead in Gauss's arms. Billy dragged his shackled legs into Garrett's office, picked up Olinger's shotgun and waited at the east window as Olinger raced back from the Wortley. Gauss cried, "Bob, the Kid has killed Bell!" Olinger looked up and said, "Yes, and he's killed me too!" as Billy called to him and shot and killed him with his own shotgun loaded with heavy buckshot. Gauss tossed Billy a pick-ax and Billy freed one leg. Billy talked to the men in front of the Wortley but warned them to not cross the street. More than an hour after the shootings, Billy managed to mount the pony Gauss brought him. Garrett later said, "He could have ridden up and down the street until dark without interference from a single resident."

After his escape, Billy rode towards Fort Stanton then veered north, crossed the river and went into the Capitan Mountain foothills. (Page 116)

WALKER, Dale     *LEGENDS AND LIES* Tom Doherty Associates, Books, New York NY 1997

After killing Bell and Olinger, Billy rode out of town burdened with his leg-iron chain dangling and with side-arms and rifle from the armory. Instead of heading for Mexico, he rode to Fort Sumner, where he had a girlfriend and several pals. He made no effort to conceal his whereabouts.    (Page 122)

## Comments
### By Charles O. Sanders

*The below comments by history researcher Charles O. Sanders reflect upon the many discrepancies or plain errors of fact by various authors who wrote about Billy over the past hundred years, as illustrated by the two overview pieces compiled by Robert Sproull in this issue: a.) Theories of How Billy Escaped; and b.) The Route He Took When he Escaped.*

*Jose Cordoba, courtesy photo*

Descendents of Jose Cordoba say the proper spelling of his name is Cordoba, rather than Cordova. With Spanish words and names, the v and b are pronounced the same; therefore, they are often interchangeable.

There was only one Jose Cordoba/ Cordova recorded as residing in Las Tablas in the 1880 United States Federal Census. On 25 June 1880, the census enumerator recorded his occupation as "Justice of the Peace." That enumerator was Sheriff George Kimball/ Kimbrell. Jose Cordoba's occupation was recorded as "farmer" in the 1870 United States Federal Census and in the 1885 New Mexico Territorial Census. I have found nothing that suggests he was ever a schoolteacher or schoolmaster. He also never had a son named Manuel (to help him remove Billy's shackles, said

some). I find it hard to believe that a JP would help Billy remove his shackles right after he had killed two law officers. I also find it unlikely that Billy would have gone running to a JP for that kind of assistance.

Various authors also made references to Celsa Gutierrez, sister of Pat Garrett's wife. Why would Billy rush to see Celsa, and expect her to be happy to see him, perhaps even help him, right after he had killed two of her brother-in-law's deputies? A Billy wannabe, Brushy, had claimed Celsa was one of his "sweethearts." He also claimed that Celsa's brother, Saval Gutierrez, went up to Canaditas and got Celsa for him. What Brushy and his biographers didn't know was that Saval/Sabal Gutierrez was Celsa's <u>husband</u>, not her brother. Saval and Celsa had been married for seven years when Billy escaped, and then had two children, and at least three afterwards. The portion of Billy tales involving Celsa is folklore at best, and originated in Texas, not New Mexico.

Authors should have focused on original primary source material/documentation. That would be like those would-be authors published before Burns, who had some semi-first-hand knowledge about what they wrote, like Hough who, in 1883, wrote about his chat with Gauss – even though he was bored by Gauss' Billy stories, and had obviously forgotten details by the time he wrote them in 1901. Later authors based their versions of the events in the courthouse and the route of BTK's escape on a handful of early accounts—primarily Garrett's, Gauss', and the newspaper stories reporting it. Authors would have been more accurate presenting what the original sources said. Except for those who <u>manufactured</u> their own primary source material, authors wrote essentially the same thing.

Editor's Note: *Sanders believes that writers of history should not paraphrase what original characters had said or the earliest writers of events had written based upon first-hand knowledge. He is convinced that facts of history are distorted when retold down through the generations, unless later writers use direct quotes from history's original witnesses.*

**Addendum to list of Theories of the Billy the Kid Escape from Lincoln**
**Submitted by Charles O. Sanders**

## VIOLENCE IN LINCOLN COUNTY, 1869-1881
**By William Aloysius Keleher**
**University of New Mexico Press,**
**Albuquerque New Mexico, 1957**
[Pages 338 -339] [Excerpt of Godfrey Gauss story published in The Lincoln County Leader on January 15, 1890]

That memorable day I came out of my room, whence I had gone to light my pipe, and was crossing the yard behind the courthouse, somebody hurrying down stairs, and deputy-sheriff Bell emerging from the door running toward me. He ran right into my arms, expired the same moment, and I laid him down, dead.

That I was in a hurry to secure assistance, or perhaps to save myself, everybody will believe. When I arrived at the garden gate leading to the street, in front of the court house, I saw the other deputy-sheriff, Olinger, coming out of the hotel opposite, with the other four or five county prisoners where they had taken their dinner. I called upon him to come quick. He did so leaving the prisoners in front of the hotel. When he had come close up to me, and while standing not more than a yard apart, I told him that I was just after laying Bell dead on the ground in the yard behind.

Before he could reply, he was struck by a well directed shot fired from a window above us, and fell dead at my feet. I ran for my life to reach my room and safety, when Billy the Kid called to me: "Don't run, I wouldn't hurt you—I am alone, and master not only of the courthouse, but also the town, for I will allow nobody to come near us."

"You go," he said, "and saddle one of Judge Leonard's horses, and I will clear out as soon as I can have the shackles loosened from my legs." With a little prospecting pick I had thrown to him through the window he was working for at least an hour, and could not accomplish more than free one leg. He came to the conclusion to await a better chance, tie one shackle to his waist-belt and started out.

Meanwhile I had saddled a small skittish pony belonging to Billy Burt, as there was no other horse available, and had also, by Billy's command, tied a pair of red blankets behind the saddle. I came near forgetting to say, that whilst I was busy saddling, and Mr. Billy Kid trying hard to get his shackles off, my partner, Sam Wortley, appeared in the door leading from the garden where he had been at work, into the yard, and that when he saw the two sheriffs lying dead he did not know whether to go in or retreat, but on the assurance of Billy the Kid that he would not hurt him he went in and made himself generally useful.

When Billy went down stairs at last, on passing the body of Bell, he said, "I'm sorry I had to kill him but couldn't help it." On passing the body of Olinger he gave him the tip of his boot, saying "You are not going to round me up again."

We went out together where I had tied up the pony, and he told me to tell the owner of same, Billy Burt, that he would send it back the next day. I, for my part, didn't much believe in his promise, but, sure enough, next morning, the pony arrived safe and sound, trailing a long lariat, at the courthouse in Lincoln.

**Another Addendum to add to the Theories of Billy the Kid's Escape**
**Submitted by Charles O. Sanders**

## THE AUTHENTIC LIFE OF BILLY, THE KID,
**By PAT. F. GARRETT, SHERIFF OF LINCOLN CO., N. M.**
**SANTA FE, NEW MEXICO;**
**New Mexican Printing and Publishing Co. 1882 [Pages 128 - 130]**

On the evening of April 28, 1881, Olinger took all the other prisoners across the street to supper, leaving Bell in charge of The Kid, in the guard room. We have but The Kid's tale, and the sparse information elicited from Mr. Geiss [sic Gauss], a German employed about the building, to determine facts in regard to events immediately following Olinger's departure. From circumstances, indications, information from Geiss [Gauss], and The Kid's admissions, the popular conclusion is that:

At The Kid's request, Bell accompanied him down stairs and into the back corral. As they returned, Bell allowed The Kid to get considerably in advance. As The Kid turned on the landing of the stairs, he was hidden from Bell. He was light and active, and, with a few noiseless bounds, reached the head of the stairs, turned to the right, put his shoulder to the door of the room used as an armory, (though locked, this door was well known to open by a firm push), entered, seized a six-shooter, returned to the head of the stairs just as Bell faced him on the landing of the staircase, some twelve steps beneath, and fired. Bell turned, ran out into the corral and towards the little gate. He fell dead before reaching it. The Kid ran to the window at the south end of the hall, saw Bell fall, then slipped his handcuffs over his hands, threw them at the body, and said: "Here, d—n you, take these, too." He then ran to my office and got a double-barreled shot-gun. This gun was a very fine one, a breechloader, and belonged to Olinger. He had loaded it that morning, in presence of the Kid, putting eighteen-buckshot in each barrel, and remarked: "The man that gets one of those loads will feel it." The Kid then entered the guard-room and stationed himself at the east window, opening on the yard.

Olinger heard the shot and started back across the street, accompanied by L. M. Clements. Olinger entered the gate leading into the yard, as Geiss [Gauss] appeared at the little corral gate and said, "Bob, The Kid has killed Bell." At the same instant The Kid's voice was heard above: "Hello, old boy," said he. "Yes, and he's killed me, too," exclaimed Olinger, and fell dead, with eighteen-buckshot in his right shoulder breast and side. The Kid went back through the guard-room, through my office, into the hall and out on the balcony. From here he could see the body of Olinger, as it lay in the projecting corner of the yard, near the gate. He took deliberate aim and fired the other barrel, the charge taking effect in nearly the same place as the first; then breaking the gun across the railing of the balcony, he threw the pieces at Olinger, saying: "Take it, d—n you, you won't follow me any more with that gun." He then returned to the back room, armed himself with a Winchester and two revolvers. He was still encumbered with his shackles, but hailing old man Geiss [Gauss], he commanded him to bring a file. Geiss [Gauss] did so, and threw it up to him in the window. The Kid then ordered the old man to go and saddle a horse that was in the stable, the property of Billy Burt, Deputy Clerk of Probate, then went to a front window, commanding a view of the street, seated himself and filed the shackles from one leg. Bob Brookshire came out on the street from the hotel opposite, and started down towards the plaza. The Kid brought his Winchester down on him and said: "Go back, young fellow, go back. I don't want to hurt you, but I am fighting for my life. I don't want to see anybody leave that house."

In the meantime, Geiss was having trouble with the horse, which broke loose and ran around the corral and yard a while, but was at last brought to the front of the house. The Kid was all over the building, on the porch, and watching from the windows. He danced about the balcony, laughed and shouted as though he had not a care on earth. He remained at the house for nearly an hour after the killing, before he made a motion to leave. As he approached to mount, the horse again broke loose and ran down towards the Rio Bonito. The Kid called to Andrew Nimley, a prisoner, who was standing by, to go and catch him. Nimley hesitated, but a quick, imperative motion by The Kid started him. He brought the horse back and The Kid remarked: "Old fellow, if you hadn't gone for this horse I would have killed you." And now he mounted and said to those in hearing: "Tell Billy Burt I will send his horse back to him," then galloped away, the shackles still hanging to one leg. He was armed with a Winchester and two revolvers. He took the road west, leading to Fort Stanton, but turned north about four miles from town, and rode in the direction of Las Tablas.

It is in order to again visit the scene of

this tragedy. It was found that Bell was hit under the right arm, the ball passing through the body and coming out under the left arm. On examination it was evident that The Kid had made a very poor shot, for him, and his hitting Bell at all was a scratch. The ball had bit the wall on Bell's right, caromed, passed through his body and buried itself in an adobe on his left. There was other proof besides the marks in the wall. The ball had surely been indented and creased before it entered the body, as these scars were filled with flesh. The Kid afterwards told Peter Maxwell that Bell shot at him twice and just missed him. There is no doubt but this statement was false. One other shot was heard before Olinger appeared on the scene, but it is believed to have been an accidental one by The Kid whilst prospecting with the arms. Olinger was shot in the right shoulder, breast and side. He was literally riddled by thirty-six buckshot.

## BILLY'S ESCAPE ROUTE FROM LINCOLN
## CONDENSATION OF VARIOUS AUTHORS' VERSIONS
### Compiled by Robert Sproull

| | |
|---|---|
| 9 April, 1881 | Billy convicted of murdering Sheriff Brady. |
| 15 April, 1881 | Judge Bristol orders Billy to be executed on 13 May and Billy starts for Lincoln. |
| 21 April, 1881 | Billy arrives in Lincoln. |
| 28 April, 1881 | Billy escapes from the Lincoln County Courthouse by killing Bell and Olinger. |
| 14 July, 1881 | Garrett shoots Billy at Fort Sumner. |

As previously stated, these are listed in alphabetical order only, NOT in order of historical value.

ANAYA, PACO          I Buried Billy
The early West Creative Pub. Co., College Station, TX   1991 Pages 56 to 65

Rode two and a half miles toward Ft. Stanton until the road to Fresquez (Salazar) Ranch, south side of the Capitan Mountains. There he was fed and the shackles were removed. Left for friend's home at Las Tablas. (Called him Petronilla; correct name was Higinio Salazar.)
Had friend, Bob Davis, get him a good horse. Left for Ft. Sumner, after being given food to take with him. Says the date was 12 May, 1881. Traveled 10 miles and turned toward Las Palas. Rode through woods and brush.
Don Casimiro gave him shelter for the night. Sent Casimiro into Lincoln to buy two boxes of .44 shells. Casimiro returned at sunset and told him that there was a big hullabaloo over the killing of the guards. Left on the 14th for the Ranch of Varela in Los Conejos. His horse got away that night. Left his saddle and blanket on a mesquite, took his rifle and headed for Ft. Sumner.

ANDERSON, RON
William Bonney *alias* Billy the Kid

Rink Press, Tumacacore, AZ   1978
Pages 65 to 66 (Designated as Fiction based on facts.)
At twilight Billy was at the home of Jose Cordova, a teacher. Jose and neighbor Sepio Salazar cut the rivets and removed Billy's shackles. Billy walks over Capitans to home of 'Luis' (Higinio) Salazar at Las Tablas. Leaves guns hanging on a tree part way. Hides out in the brush. Higinio brings him food. The kid and 'Luis" steal prize horse, Don, from the Block ranch. Won't go to Mexico. Has to see Celsa, Garrett's wife's sister.
Billy started before dawn and rode at slow pace all day. At twilight he picked up the pace. At midnight still going under a full moon. (It was a new moon.) Knew where the water holes were. He rested at dawn and then made his way to Fort Sumner and Celsa.

BALLERT, MARION &  BREIHAN, CARL W.
Billy the Kid. A Date with Destiny.
Superior Publishing Co., Seattle, WA   1970
Pages 116-117

Galloped west out of Lincoln some miles and took the first trail to the right through the

Capitans. Went to home of his friend Jose Cordova. Arrived at twilight. Cordova sent a boy to get Sepio Salazar to help him remove the leg irons. (Billy never told who had done this.)

Proceeded to Higinio Salazar's home and spent the night. Early next morning Billy left on Nolan Richardson's horse, Don, for Ft. Sumner—100 miles away. Slow pace during the heat of the day. Swiftly after dusk had cooled the desert. Don was winded and was left at a ranch at Lake Thule, 30 miles east of Ft. Sumner according to Francisco Lovato.

John Meadows, many years later, says he met Billy after the escape at a cabin where he and Tom Norris were living on the banks of the Penasco. Meadows owed Billy a favor for Billy's care when Meadows needed help when he arrived at Ft. Sumner broke and blistered in 1879.

**BALLOW, WILLARD**     Billy the Kid.
A Graphic History. Owlhoot Trail Publishing Co., Ft. Worth, TX.   1998 Pages 131 to 136.

Billy left Lincoln riding West. Four miles up the valley he turned north off the main road, across the Rio Bonito and into Salazar Canyon to the home of Jose Cordova, a teacher and horse thief. He was fed and another friend, Scipio Salazar, helped remove the shackles from his legs. Billy would not stay for but pushed on for Las Tablas. (According to Ballow he took long route through Capitan gap.) Shortly after daybreak he arrived at Las Tablas where he hid in the brush and slept most of the day.

Salazar fed Billy and then they hid outside and talked. The next day he returned Burt's horse. Billy stayed at Las Tablas for three more days hiding out and sleeping. He then stole a horse from a nearby ranch and headed northeast toward Ft. Sumner, traveling only at night.

On May 6th two cowboys scared Billy's horse when he was 20 miles from Fort Sumner so Billy stole a horse from Montgomery Bell. Bell reported it missing to Barney Mason and Jim Cureton. Billy admitted to having the horse but said he'd pay for it or return it. (Barney Mason fled when he learned it was Billy who had taken the horse. "Wore the sight off his pistol using it as a quirt!)

**BARKER, ALLEN**   The Kid With Fast Hands
Pine Grove, CA  1993  History w/ fictional dialogue.  Page 394.

Trotted west out of Lincoln. Turned north at the mouth of Salazar Canyon. Stopped at Jose Cordovo's ranch before dark. Slept in the brush. The next day he  had the leg irons removed by Jose and Sepio Salazar. Rode to Ygenio Salazar's home in Las Tablas. Stole a horse from Brady (sic) Richardson of the Block Ranch. Rode across Conejo Mesa to Ft. Sumner.

**BRANCH, LOUIS LEON**   "Los Billitos": The Story of "Billy the Kid" & His Gang.
Carlton Press, Inc., NY, NY   1980

From Lincoln rode west toward Ft. Stanton, and north through Baca Canyon toward the ranch of a friend, Juan Padilla. Left horse there and went by foot up canyon to Jose Cordova's home, a few miles to the west. Cordova and his son, Manuel, helped remove the heavy leg shackles. Billy's leg was bleeding but he would not stay overnight. Started for Ygenio Salazar's as he feared Garrett and a posse would be close behind.

Near exhaustion, Billy staggered to Ygenio's place at Las Tablas and arrived late at night; welcomed exuberantly by Ygenio and his wife. Early next morning Billy left for Ft. Sumner, 90 miles from Las Tablas as the crow flies, on a horse borrowed or stolen from the Block Ranch.

After the escape on 28 April nothing was known of him until rumors placed him at cow and sheep camps around Ft. Sumner, Mesilla or Arenosa.

**BRENT, WILLIAM**
The Complete and Factual Life of Billy the Kid.
Frederick Fell Inc., NY  1964  Pages 182 -183

Pat tried to trail Billy but could not. Billy Burt's horse came back with blood on the saddle. The blood was put there by Billy from a jackrabbit he killed. He told this to Pete Maxwell and Jesus Leiva later at Ft. Sumner over a beer. Billy was reported to have been at Las Tablas where he had stolen a horse from Andy Richardson. He stole another from Montgomery

Bell near Ft. Sumner. Billy was reported to have been seen at Las Canaditas and Arenoso.

BRUNS, ROGER A. Billy the Kid. Outlaw of the Wild West. Enslow Publishers, Inc., Berkeley Heights, NJ 2000. Page 90

Bruns repeats the story that Billy placed two pistols and cartridge belts in the fork of an Oak tree to lighten his load while climbing the Capitans. He did not get back to retrieve them.

BURNS, WALTER NOBLE
The Saga of Billy the Kid.
Doubleday, Page & Co., New York, NY 1926
Pages 254 to 261

Billy rode due west out of Lincoln and turned north-by-west into Baca road and over the Baca ford. He went to the adobe jacal of Jesus Jose Padilla who fed him and gave him coffee. Billy sent Burt's horse back with a note tied to the cantle. Billy walked westward and arrived early in the morning at the goat ranch of Jose Cordoba who had a wayside smithy. Jose and his helper, Benito Rodriguez, removed the leg shackles. Billy would not stay but pushed on for his friend, Ighenio Salazar in Las Tablas and arrived there at night under a shining half moon. As he ate a meal prepared by Salazar' wife, Billy told Salazar he grabbed Bell's gun as they played cards and when Bell ran down the stairs he was forced to kill him. Billy stayed at Las Tablas for two days, and according to Burns, rode out on a horse borrowed from Andy Richardson by Jose Jorado.

COE, GEORGE W. Frontier Fighter
Houghton, Mifflin Co., NY, NY 1934
Page 153-154

A horse was brought to Billy after the chain between the leg shackles was severed and Billy tied the ends to his belt. After being thrown he re-mounted and rode out of Lincoln. His first stop was with Ygenio Salazar's home where he sent the horse back to Lincoln. He cautiously called Ygenio who fed him. He refused to stay telling Ygenio he had to go to Fort Sumner to see his best girl.

CRAMER, T. DUDLEY The Pecos Ranchers in the Lincoln County War. Branding Iron Press, Oakland, CA 1996 Page 169

The kid stayed about an hour chatting with people in front of the Wortley and then rode north out of town, unchallenged! Everyone thought he would leave the state immediately. But the first night he stayed at the goat ranch of his friend Jose Cordova in the Capitan foothills. He let his horse loose and borrowed another horse to ride over the Capitans to Las Tablas and his friend, Ygenio Salazar where he stayed for three days. He then rode northeast to the Fort Sumner area and for two and one half months he moved from sheep camp to sheep camp with occasional visits to one of his girlfriends in Fort Sumner.

CURRY, GEORGE
An Autobiography. University of NM Press, Albuquerque, NM 1958 Page 43

After escaping, Billy rode out of Lincoln on Billy Burt's horse. Went up the Rio Bonito, through Baca Canyon and through a gap in the Capitan Mountains to Las Tablas. Stopped at Eugenio Salazar's home and sent Burt's horse back with a boy. Remained at Salazar's home for two days. Stole Andy Richardson's horse from the Block Ranch and went to Ft. Sumner.

FULTON, MAURICE G. History of the Lincoln County War University of Arizona Press, Tuscon, AZ 1968 Page 397

Departure from Lincoln was unhampered. A short ride brought him to the nearby Capitan foothills where he spent the night at the goat-ranch home of his friend, schoolmaster Jose Cordova. Released his mount and the next morning Billy set to work to rid himself of the remaining leg iron. He borrowed another horse and saddle, this time with the owner's willing consent, and headed for Ft. Sumner.

GADDY, JERRY J. Obituaries of the Gun Fighters. Dust to Dust.
Presidio Press, San Rafael, CA 1977

The young monster stepped out on the portico of the old house and defied the whole town. (After killing Bell & Olinger) he made one man knock his irons off, and covering another with his death dealing shot-gun, ordered him to saddle a horse that was standing on the street, walked out, mounted and galloped out of town in the presence of the whole population.

GARRETT, PAT F.     The Authentic Life of Billy the Kid.  The Macmillan Company, New York, NY   1927 Edited by Maurice G. Fulton. Page 206-207

Rode out of Lincoln, on Billy Burt's horse, west toward Ft. Stanton but turned north after 4 miles toward Las Tablas. (Billy Burt's horse showed up in Lincoln a few days later dragging a rope.)

Stole a horse from Andy Richardson at the Block Ranch and rode it to within a few miles of Ft. Sumner. The horse got away and Billy walked into Ft. Sumner. At Ft. Sumner he stole a horse from Montgomery Bell and rode it bareback, going south. Bell got Barney Mason and Curington to get the horse back from what he thought were Mexican thieves. When they got to a Mexican camp, Billy stepped out and Barney Mason fled. Curington talked to Billy who said he would pay Bell or send the horse back.

HENDRON, J.   The Story of Billy the Kid. Rydal Press, Santa Fe, NM   1948 Pages 27, 28

Billy…mounted the horse Goss (sic) had saddled, stuck the Winchester in the scabbard and left. Everyone at Lincoln witnessed the exodus. About four miles west of Lincoln a trail cut to the north, crossed the Rio Bonito and went through the gap. Billy stopped at Pablo Fresca's *rancho* long enough to eat a bite and have Pablo file off his leg irons. At the foot of the Capitans the Kid slapped his horse and sent it trotting back to Lincoln. *It was almost dark* when he stopped for the night.

The next day (29 April) he began his long journey. When he reached the top of the mountain he turned and went into Capitan Gap where he found a one-room shelter. The Kid remained here until dawn when he took to the open, hiding in the shadows of scrubby growth.

In the distance was the *jacal* of Jose Jorado, a longtime friend and the brother-in-law of the dead Charlie Bowdre. Petronillo Sedillo, another friend, lived close by. The Kid remained there that night and all the next day.

The next night, April 30, Petronillo summoned Bob Davis from the Block Ranch. Davis brought a horse and saddle for the Kid who in a short time was loping his mount toward the Ft. Sumner road. (To throw off pursuit) Billy turned south eight miles to the small village of Las Palas where Casemide Biyesca lived and was hidden for the night. On April 31 (sic) Casemide went into Lincoln, and reported to Billy that Garrett was going to kill Billy if he found him. He advised Billy to go to Mexico. Billy ignored the advice, crossed the salt flat, and went over the mesa to the Ciengo de Macho and spent the night. His horse broke loose and he was again afoot. He walked the 18 miles to Cibola on the Rio Pecos where Jesus Anaya lived. By day Billy stayed in the house. At night he slept in a cave 300 yards away. On a morning in early June he went on to Ft. Sumner.

HUNT, FRAZIER   The Tragic Days of Billy the Kid. Hasting House Publishers, New York, NY, 1956   Page 288 to 298

Billy rode west toward Ft. Stanton. Worried about the Apache trackers at Mescalero Indian Agency helping Garrett, not about the troopers. Turned right on the first trail that wound its way through the gap in the Capitans. Stopped at home of Jose Cordova. Cordova and neighbor Sepio Salazar removed the leg irons. Went to Ygenio Salazar's home as it was growing dark. Salazar helped Billy steal Don, a racehorse belonging to Andy Richardson, from the Block Ranch.

Left for FT. Sumner, 100 miles away. Knew all the water holes.

JOHNSON, JIM   Billy the Kid. His Real Name Was… Outskirts Press, Inc., Denver, CO 2006
"There are various versions of what happened after Bonney left Lincoln, but the following is the most widely accepted version," claimed the author.

Billy rode west and then north through a canyon to the ranch of his friend, Juan Padilla, where he left the horse. Then walked to Jose Cordova's house a few miles to the west. Cordova and his son, Manuel, helped Bonney remove the shackles. Would not stay overnight for fear of a posse. Late that night arrived at the house of his friend, Ygenio Salazar near Las Tablas on the north side of the Capitans and spent a few days there. Ygenio got a part mustang and quarter horse for Billy that belonged to Andrew Richardson of the Block Ranch.

Billy first headed south to fool pursuers and arrived at the ranch of John Meadows and Tom Norris. Meadows advised him to go to Mexico but for some reason Billy refused and said he was going to Ft. Sumner. Reasons? Perhaps a girl friend. Maybe because that would be the last place they would look for him. Perhaps to plan revenge on Garrett, Chisum and Mason.

On May 7, Billy walked into Ft. Sumner. His horse had gotten away. He stayed with various friends.

KELEHER, WILLIAM A. Violence in Lincoln County University of NM Press, Albuquerque, NM 1957 Pages 339-340

Rode east down the road from Lincoln until he reached the home of Higinio Salazar. With a file and other tools furnished by Salazar, he removed the leg irons. He then struck off cross country toward the Pecos and Ft. Sumner, a pathway known ever since as the "Bonney Escape Trail."

NOLAN, FREDERICK The Lincoln County War. A Documentary History. University of Oklahoma Press, Norman, OK 1992 Page 420

Billy rode out of Lincoln on Billy Burt's pony, stopping at Ygenio Salazar's house west of town where his friend helped him remove the leg shackles. Ygenio rustled up a good horse for Billy, a prize bay named Don, belonging to Andy Richardson. He did not go south but instead returned to his old hangouts around Ft. Sumner. He told Meadows that he had no money and he had many friends at Ft. Sumner.

NOLAN, FREDERICK The West of Billy the Kid University of Oklahoma Press, Norman, OK 1998 Pages 276-277

A Barney Mason interview in the *Las Vegas Gazette* said Billy went first to or about the Agua Azul in the Capitan Mountains where he lost the horse taken in Lincoln. (Ygenio Salazar confirmed this saying that Billy came to Las Tablas, a few miles from Agua Azul and "laid off there for three or four days…out in the hills and came to my house to eat. I told him to leave this place and go to old Mexico." While at Las Tablas Billy Burt's pony got loose and went back to Lincoln.)

"He went from there down about Newcomb's cow camp (on the Feliz)" said Barney Mason in his interview. "There he took a horse from one of his men and rode to Consios (Conejos) Springs (about 20 miles southwest of Fort Sumner). There he slept again." This correlates more or less with John Meadow's claim that the Kid came to see him at his Penasco Ranch and gave him his account of the escape. Meadows also urged him to go to Mexico but Billy said he first had to get some money.

Mason continued in his interview: "Currington (Jim Cureton) was rounding up cattle (at Conejos Springs) ….and woke the sleeping Billy." When Billy jumped up he scared his horse which broke away and escaped. He footed it to Buffalo Arroyo, about 12 miles, where he was furnished with another horse. From there he made his way to Ft. Sumner by the west side of the river. "He staid [sic] above Ft. Sumner that evening."

OTERO, MIGUEL ANTONIO The Real Billy the Kid Rufus Rockwell Wilson, Inc., NY, NY. 1936 Pages 186-187.

Billy remained in the building nearly an hour before he attempted to mount Billy Burt's horse, got thrown, remounted and rode out of town after telling the crowd he would send the horse back. He was armed with a Winchester and two revolvers and rode in the direction of Las Tablas. The Kid returned Burt's horse and stole another one from Andy Richardson at Las Tablas and headed for Ft. Sumner. The horse got away outside Ft. Sumner, so Billy walked the rest of the way. He tried to get his sweetheart to run away with him to Mexico but her mother was sick and she refused to go.

RUDOLF, CHARLES F.   Los Billitos. The story of BTK and his gang.  As told to: BRANCH, LOUIS LEON A Hearthstone Book, Carlton Press, NY NY   1980    Pages 243 to 244

After the escape, Billy rode west toward Ft. Stanton and then turned north through Baca Canyon. Stopped at Juan Padilla's and rested. Left horse with Padilla to return. Walked to Jose Cordova's several miles to the west. Shackles removed.  Would not stay for the night. Went to Ygenio's home in Las Tablas. Arrived late at night. Stole horse from Andy Richardson and left for Fort Sumner to see Celsa.

SCHUMARD, GEORGE    Billy the Kid. The Robin Hood of Lincoln County.  Mesilla Old Times, Mesilla, NM  1969   Page 40

After his escape, Billy rode west toward FT. Stanton then north through Baca Canyon toward Juan Padilla's ranch. Rested. Left his horse.  Went on foot to Jose Cordova's place several miles to the west. ( Author doubts Billy would have left his horse as a posse could have been on his trail.) At Cordova's, Cordova and his helper removed the leg irons and gave Billy directions to Ygenio Salazar's home. Reached Salazar's home after dark in Las Tablas, a small Mexican community nestled in the foothills of the Capitan Mountains.

Probably told Salazar the complete story of the escape' but Salazar was always reluctant to talk about it.

SONNICHSEN, C. L. & MORRISON, Wm. V. Alias Billy the Kid    University of New Mexico Press, Albuquerque, NM   1955   Pages 45-47

Bill said, "I got on the horse and rode out of Lincoln to the west and up the canyon to the home of a friend, who cut the bolts in my leg irons. After they screwed the nuts on the bolts, they riveted over the ends of the bolts so I could unscrew them with my hands." (In a footnote Sonnichsen says that the adopted daughter of Higinio Salazar told Morrison that Higinio's

cousin, Sepio Salazar, was the one who cut the bolts and hid the irons.)

He continued: "I turned the horse back for Lincoln and walked over the mountain." He said the guns got heavy so he hung them on a fork of a tree. He went to Higinio's home in Las Tablas and Higinio came outside when he whistled. He brought him a blanket and he slept in the underbrush. The next day he brought him food. "On the second day he borrowed a horse and I started for Ft Sumner across the plains." "While on the way the horse broke loose and left me on foot again. I walked into Anaya's sheep camp below Ft. Sumner and stayed a few days. I traveled by night and slept in the daytime."

TUSKA, JON     Billy the Kid. A Handbook University Of Nebraska Press, Lincoln, Nebraska Page 100

Billy rode the short distance to the foothills of the Capitan Mountains and spent the night at the goat ranch of his friend, Jose Cordova, a schoolmaster. He released Billy Burt's pony and worked to rid himself of the remaining leg iron. He borrowed a horse and saddle from Cordova, with Cordova's consent, and rode toward Ft. Sumner.

When he attended the Roswell Old-Timers Meeting in 1931, John Meadows recalled meeting Billy. "The Kid came to my place three or four days after his  escape from jail." He and Tom Norris were at his ranch. Meadows had been grateful for Billy's help when he was sick, and offered him some Indian ponies. Advised Billy to leave the country. Billy said he needed money to live on before he left.

UTLEY, ROBERT M.        Billy the Kid. University of Nebraska Press, Lincoln, Nebraska 1989.  Pages 182 to 185

After his escape, Billy rode towards Ft. Stanton and then veered north, crossed the river and went into the Capitan Mountain foothills. Had coffee with goat's milk served by Francisco Gomez at the home of Ataviano Salas. Rode to the home of Jose Cordova in Salazar Canyon where the shackles were removed by Cordova and Sepio Salazar. Headed up the canyon toward Capitan Summit, aiming for Las Tablas on the other side of the mountain to the home of Ygenio

Salazar. Stayed three days. Stole a horse and headed east, circling the north base of the Capitans to Aqua Azul. Then headed south, crossed the Ruidoso above San Patricio and made his way to the Penasco and John Meadows.

The next day Billy headed for Ft. Sumner. Several days later at Conejos Springs his horse spooked. He hiked 20 miles to Ft. Sumner. He reached Ft. Sumner on Saturday, May 7th, nine days after his Lincoln escape. It was that night that he found the tethered horse belonging to Montgomery Bell, a rancher from 50 miles south, and rode away bareback. Bell reported the theft to deputy sheriff Barney Mason and that was how Cureton and Mason came upon Billy…and Barney fled!

Additional notes to Chapter 17  Page 265
Gomez incorrectly remembers the escape at noon instead of evening. Has Billy going up Baca Canyon rather than Salazar Canyon which is the logical route over the mountain to Las Tablas. Salazar Canyon would have had Billy reach Capitan Summit near the head of Las Tablas Creek.

WALLIS, MICHAEL  Billy the Kid. The Endless Ride.  W. W. Norton & Co., New York.  2007 Page 245

Billy left Lincoln on the horse of Billy Burt, the deputy court clerk. The horse returned the next day dragging a halter rope. The Kid rode over the Capitan Mountains and stayed with several Hispanic friends, including Ygenio Salazar. All his friends urged him to leave the country, but he refused even after Wallace posted another $500 reward for the Kid's capture before he departed for Turkey.

# Dr. Robert C. Sproull

## By Jan Girand

*Bob Sproull photo by Jan Girand*

Dr. Robert "Bob" Sproull lives in El Paso, Texas with his wife of 63 years, Peggy. Born in 1920 in West Virginia, he grew up in the tiny town of Chicora in western Pennsylvania. He served 30 years in the military and a total of 46 years practicing dentistry, most of that time in the specialized field of Prosthodontics. As an enlisted man, Bob served 39 months during World War II in the 80th Infantry Division, Patton's Third Army, which saw savage combat. In both WWII and Korea, where he was a dental officer, he served under direct enemy fire. He retired in 1973 as a Bird Colonel. He continued in private practice for another 23 years.

He was honorably discharged after the Second World War, and enrolled in dental school at the University of Pittsburgh. After graduation, he volunteered to be commissioned in the Army and remained in that service for a total of 30 years. During that period he received his specialty training and was certified by the American Board of Prosthodontics as a Diplomate of that specialty. Because of his roles as clinician, researcher, teacher and lecturer, he was in constant demand and was known as one of the finest prosthodontists in the Army. He educated seven residents and more than forty interns in that field. During his years of study and practice, he pioneered the application of color science to the matching of the color of natural teeth. His work resulted in the spectrophotometric analysis of natural tooth enamel and the materials used in dentistry to duplicate those colors. In 2009, at nearly 90, Bob was the honored keynote speaker at the Annual Session of *The Society for Color and Appearance in Dentistry* held in Houston, Texas. The SCAD is an International Organization; their membership includes color experts from around the world. He was the first recipient of the Society's top honor, The Bruce Clark Award.

Since his retirement, Bob has applied his state-of-the art metallurgy artistry and tools to various hobbies. He has made countless little Billy the Kid figures in lead-free pewter and other unique pieces of art, many of them humorous, for appreciative recipients. With his metal detector and friends in the Prospectors Club of El Paso, he continues his historical and treasure seeking hobby, begun while he was stationed in West Germany. (He assisted the German Archaeologist of the Kurphalziches Museum, Dr. Berndmark Heukemes, during that four year tour in Heidelberg.)

He and his wife have an amazing art collection and an extensive library of southwestern history. Because he has read and digested all of those books on his shelves, authors and other researchers often call upon him to provide them with historical information. He has been an invaluable resource for the editor of *PastWord*.

*Robert Sproull, circa 2009, seems to look back on himself in 1942. Photo magic by Charles O. Sanders.*

## What is a prosthodontist, you ask?

From this link: *http://www.prosthodontics.org/aboutus/prosthodontics.asp* … comes the following excerpt: "Prosthodontists provide an extremely high level of care to patients with missing teeth, or having significant damage to their existing teeth. Prosthodontists work with congenital defects as well as problems arising from trauma and neglect. Prosthodontists are highly trained in state-of-the-art techniques and procedures for treating many diverse and complex dental conditions and restoring optimum function and esthetics. These include: crowns, bridges, complete and removable partial dentures, dental implants, TMD-jaw joint problems, traumatic injuries to the mouth's structure and/or teeth, snoring or sleep disorders and oral cancer reconstruction and continuing care."

And in the case of Bob Sproull during his active war years, it also involved him, beginning on the battlefield, in the care of soldiers' traumatic injuries to the mouth's structure and teeth.

## BRONCO SUE IN THE NEWS

Also known as Susan Warfield, Susie Raper,
Susan Stone, Sue Yonkers and Sue Dawson.

### Compiled by Charles O. Sanders

THE OWYHEE AVALANCHE, Silver City,
Idaho Territory, Saturday, March 5, 1870:
ELKO ITEMS. - From the Independent of
February 23d:

On Monday last Susie Raper, having been
released from confinement on bail, was
immediately recommitted on a charge of theft of
jewelry.

SACRAMENTO DAILY UNION, Sacramento,
California, Monday, March 14, 1870:

SUSIE RAPER, indicted in Elko county,
Nevada, for cattle stealing, has been tried and
acquitted.
THE OWYHEE AVALANCHE, Silver City,
Idaho Territory, Saturday, March 19, 1870:
ELKO ITEMS. - From the Independent of last
Saturday:

Susie Raper, charged with stealing a band
of Cattle, was acquitted.

A. Huggan was on the defense of Susie
Raper. He is making his mark in Elko.

THE OWYHEE AVALANCHE, Silver City,
Idaho Territory, Saturday, March 26, 1870:
ELKO ITEMS. - From the Independent of
March 19th:

Susie Raper indicted for grand larceny
was acquitted, thus escaping two indictments, one
for stealing cattle and one for stealing jewelry.

CINCINNATI DAILY ENQUIRER, Cincinnati,
Ohio, Thursday Morning, March 31, 1870:
LADY GAY SPANKER ON THE PACIFIC.
A Handsome and Dashing Young Cattle Stealer
Among the Pacific Slopes.
[From the Sacramento (Cal.) Independent of
March 12.]

The case of Susie Raper, indicted by the
grand jury of Elko County for grand larceny for
the stealing of a band of cattle, has been on trial
for the last two days. The courtroom has been
crowded with eager spectators ever since the

opening of the case. The defendant is a woman of
about twenty-nine years of age, an Australian by
birth, is rather prepossessing in appearance, has
a passable face, a graceful and well-rounded form
and good carriage. She came to Humboldt
County at an early day, and during her residence
there ran many of its prominent citizens a merry
string.

As a coquette she has been successful in
capturing the affections and coin of many clever
but "spooney" chaps all over the country. She
has cheek enough to put up and attempt to carry
out any kind of a job. Smart, bold and of winning
ways, she seldom missed her mark. She can shoot
a pistol like a sportsman, ride a mustang with all
the grace and dash of a vaquero, drive a bull
team equal to any Missourian, and in the parlor
or ballroom "get away" with most women of
style. She was arrested on the 18th of January in
Lander County while attempting to escape, and
showed fight, nerve and skill in the handling of a
six-shooter on the occasion. She was incarcerated
in the county jail here, being unable to procure
bail. She has a husband and three boys, aged
respectively nine, seven and five years. Several
attempts were made to procure her release under
writ of habeas corpus, and when brought into the
court on these occasions she acted as if it was fun.

During this trial she sat by her able
counsel, rarely exhibiting any concern in her face,
and in passing to and from the jail has given up
the coquettish swagger that generally
characterizes her movements. When the keys
were first turned on her by the Sheriff she gave
way to her emotions, and a flood of tears gushed
freely from her hazel eyes. This lasted but a
moment, when she gave vent to a tirade of abuse
upon the heads of those who had deserted her.
After eloquent and able arguments on both sides,
the case was submitted to the jury at five o'clock
last night, which, after being out two hours,
returned a verdict of "not guilty." Another
indictment for grand larceny - stealing jewelry -
is hanging over her, upon which she will be tried
next week.

SACRAMENTO DAILY UNION, Sacramento,
California, Friday, May 13, 1870:
THE MAZEPPA OF THE HUMBOLDT. - The
Elko (Nevada), Independent of May 11th thus
refers to a noted female celebrity in that vicinity:

The town of Carlin is the home of Susie Raper, the famous Lady Gay Spanker and female buccaneer of the sagebrush. Every now and then the citizens of that place are treated to a little fun by their fair damsel. Susie has no superior in boldness, dash and intrigue, if any equals. No yellow-covered book ever pictured her equal, if all accounts are true. Susie is as gay and as festive as any female troubadour who ever trod the mountains under the blue sky of Italy. Possessing a natural and graceful appearance, a keen eye, quick intellect, a tongue that swings on a pivot, she can make up to represent any character and has ability enough to execute any deep-laid scheme. The Mazeppa chief of a gang of land pirates, she boasts of her power to command at a moment's warning, their assistance to execute her wishes, however unlawful or diabolical they may be. The experience of the dungeon taught her no lesson, as it was hoped it would have done by her lovers. On Friday last a valuable race horse of hers, named Humboldt, was attached by Constable Brophy to satisfy a butcher bill, at Mineral Hill, and brought to Carlin without her knowledge. On learning the fact she went to the stable where the horse was kept, and coaxed the groomsman to allow her to lead him into the yard to see if the animal would recognize her. No sooner was she out than she sprang astride Humboldt and started for another stable, claiming possession and threatening the officers with destruction if they attempted to retake the horse. She was finally captured, after a liberal exhibition of her well-moulded extremities to the greedy street gazers, in her Menken ride through the town. The horse was placed in a secure position, and Susie left with curses on her lips.

ALBUQUERQUE MORNING JOURNAL, Albuquerque, New Mexico, Tuesday, August 26, 1884:
The Socorro Killing.

The reporter of THE JOURNAL ran across R. B. Featherstone, or "Bob," as he is familiarly known, the town marshal of Socorro, at the Armijo house last evening.

"Have you seen the account of the Yonkers-Black killing, as given in the evening paper;" asked THE JOURNAL man.

"I have read it. It's full of blunders that ought to be corrected," answered the marshal.

"Will you be kind enough to give THE JOURNAL readers the correct version?"

"Certainly. In the first place the man's name is Robert Black and the woman's Susan Yonkers. They came to Socorro together from White Oaks about a month ago. Nobody in Socorro seemed to know anything about them or their previous history. Black opened saloon at the Walker House, while the woman kept house in the old Cartinell building down near the railroad. Black took his meals at the house, but slept at the saloon, at least until a week ago when Walker closed him out; and then he went to sleep and eat at the woman's house.

"So far as we know at Socorro," said the officer, the woman has never been dissipated, and as for her going to the saloon, that is not true, for she was never seen there. Last week Black went to Squire Kelley and deeded his ranch to the woman. Before that time she had no interest in the property.

"On Saturday last," continued the marshal, "Black was under the influence of liquor and the woman came to me and asked that he be taken away from the house. I went and brought him up town about 5 p. m. and had him registered at the hotel. Later in the evening she came to me again and this time I locked him up, but on Sunday morning two of his friends came and went his bail. I admonished him again about going near the house and he promised to stay away. About [?] o'clock Sunday the woman came and asked me if she could get into a hardware store and about an hour afterwards the hardware dealer told me he had sold her a 44-calibre bull-dog, but that he gave her cartridges that would not go into the pistol. I met Black and told him about this and he replied: You bet I won't go to the house for she is a shooter from away back. I afterwards met the woman and she wanted some cartridges from me giving as a reason that she had a lot of jewelry in the house and was afraid it would be stolen. Of course she didn't get the cartridges.

"About 4 o'clock the news came that she had killed Black and I hurried down to the house. The woman, now a murderess, had given herself up to Sheriff Simpson, who lives only a short distance from the house. She said she had killed Black after he had thrown a goblet at her and had chased her with an axe. The axe lay near the corpse, but no one knew who put it there. The woman is now in custody. The dead man had been shot through the left arm, the ball passing directly through the heart and being extracted just above the right nipple."

Robert Black is said to have been a handsome man, fully six feet in height, with heavy black moustache.

RIO GRANDE REPUBLICAN, Las Cruces, New Mexico, Saturday, December 19, 1885:
A MURDER TRIAL.
J. H. Good and Lewin McFerrin Tried for the Killing of Chas. Dawson.

Last Sunday deputy sheriff Sleese brought down from Tularosa J. H. Good and Lewin McFerrin, who had their preliminary trial here this week for the murder of Chas. Dawson. It seems that the case was called before Justice Hill, but no one appearing for the prosecution it was dismissed. Wm. Raper, step-son of the man who was killed, came to Las Cruces and made complaint, and the case occupied Monday, Tuesday and Wednesday before Justice Valdez and resulted in Good and McFerrin being bound over in the sum of $3,000 each, with C. R. Scott and Chas. Rhodius, sureties.

The case excited much attention and the court house was selected as the most comfortable and commodious quarters for holding the trial. Col. Fountain was attorney for the prosecution and Maj. Llewellyn and Col. Rynerson represented the defense.
TESTIMONY FOR THE PROSECUTION.

The wife of the deceased testified that on the morning the fight occurred she was driving in a wagon accompanied by a Negro, an American and a Mexican boy, while her husband rode behind on horseback. When about six or eight miles from La Luz they suddenly came upon Good, who was in a buggy with Mrs. Jenks. They came so close their horses' heads were together, and as soon as Good saw Dawson he handed the reins to Mrs. Jenks and picked up his Winchester rifle. The witness jumped from the wagon and ran towards Good begging him not to shoot. She said:

"Good ballowed for Dawson to come up and talk to him like a man, and said to him when he came, 'you've been talking about me.' He said: 'No, Mr. Good, I have not.' To which Good

replied, you have been writing to my wife that I was living with a woman.' My husband said he would not meet him at any place and talk it over, and Mr. Good said he would meet him at the store in town. Afterwards he said: 'Dawson, the town can't hold us both.' Then we separated."

In the afternoon a Mexican came with a note from Mr. Good, but her husband was feeding the horses and the Mexican would not give it to her. Afterwards Raper wanted Dawson to go and talk it over, and a man named Mackay came and said Good wanted to see him. Dawson said he would meet him at the house, but did not want any fighting. Mackay and Dawson went together with Wm. Raper and a boy named A. J. Burks. The witness followed behind a wall, and just as she came to an opening where she could see the parties they had just met, and the firing commenced immediately, McFerrin firing the first shot at Wm. Raper, and Good shooting at Dawson. She ran back after a rifle for her boy to protect himself with, and when she got back the fighting had ceased, and she ran and held Dawson in her arms where he died.
Raper's testimony corroborated that of his mother in all that occurred at the house and at the fight. He testified that he could not get his pistol out and did not fire a shot.

J. Burk, a young man who gave his age at 21 years, gave similar testimony. He was with Dawson and Raper when they went to meet Good's party. When they had come within two yards of each other they stopped, and Dawson extended his right hand toward Good and said: "Did you tell Mackay - ." At that McFerrin said: "Make your pledge," and fired in the direction of Raper. Good fired the next shot at Dawson, and Dawson fell. The witness then ran, drawing his pistol and fired one shot.

Cruz Duran was in the wagon when Good and Dawson met in the morning, and testified that Dawson took his Winchester from his scabbard on his saddle.
This closed the testimony for the prosecution.
TESTIMONY FOR THE DEFENSE.

Charles Rhodius, the first witness called for the defense, was sick in the house when the party left to go meet Good. He says that all were armed, and that Mrs. Dawson took a rifle and followed them saying that "if there was any trouble she would be there; if not, she would keep the rifle hid."

C. R. Scott was next called and told the story of the shooting. When the parties met they were twenty-five or thirty steps from him. He could not hear their conversation, but heard Dawson say in a loud voice, "I said it." Raper then made a pass and pulled his six-shooter, and almost the time McFerrin got his out, both fired "like that," (snapping his fingers to explain). Raper jumped back, then two more shots were fired and the firing became general. Saw Dawson with a six-shooter in his hands.

McFerrin, one of the defendants, testified that he went with Good and Mackay when they met Dawson. Some words were passed between Dawson, Mackay and Good. Raper said to the witness, "what are you doing here?" and he replied, "looking on." At the same time Raper spoke he was pulling his pistol, and witness did the same. Could not say which fired first, the shots were so close together. Raper dodged and ran off, shooting back. The young man, Burks, was standing in the road shooting at Good and witness. Dawson fired at Good. As he fired the second time Good shot him down. There was a woman coming and the witness stepped back into a hallway. When he did, Dawson was down, trying to work his pistol.

J. R. Sleese testified that Mrs. Dawson told him that she took the rifle with her when she left the house.

After his arrival here Mr. Good had Raper and Burks arrested for an assault with attempt to kill, and they were bound over in the sum of $500 each.

RIO GRANDE REPUBLICAN, Las Cruces, New Mexico, Saturday, March 13, 1886:
GRAND JURY.

William Raper was indicted by the Grand Jury, for assault with intent to kill. He was one of the participants in the Good-Dawson fracas.

The Grand Jury indicted Jno. H. Good for murder in the first degree. His counsel Rynerson, Wade and Llewellyn at once sued out a writ of habeas corpus. After hearing the testimony the Judge remanded Good to jail without bail. His case is set for trial Wednesday the 21st.

SOCORRO BULLION, Socorro, New Mexico, Saturday, April 24, 1886:
ADDITIONAL LOCALS.

Judge Brinker leaves to-night for Las Lunas. For the past two days he has been holding court in chambers in this city. Sue Yonker's bail has been fixed at $7,500.

DAILY INDEPENDENT, Elko, Nevada, Friday, May 28, 1886:
SUSIE RAPER. The Eventful Career of a Former Notorious Female Resident of Elko County.

The following from the Socorro, New Mexico, Chieftain of the 22nd instant relates to a female who will be remembered by all old residents of Elko county. She resided here for a number of years at Carlin, was connected with a band of cattle and horse thieves which infested this section in 1869 and 1870, and was for several months a prisoner in the county jail here on a charge of cattle stealing. She left here, if we remember correctly, sometime in 1871, and went to Colorado with her paramour, Captain Payne, who was afterwards sent to the penitentiary from that then territory for some offense, probably horse theft. Of her subsequent career, the Chieftain says:

"For some time past efforts have been made to obtain something of the life and character of the woman known as Sue Yonkers, now confined in the county jail charged with the murder of George Black in this city August 17th, 1884. Upon investigation we find that she is not a native of America, but was born in South Wales on the 11th day of September, 1844, and her maiden name was Susan Warfield. It is not known at what age she came to this country, but as she has relatives in New Orleans, it is believed that she landed there about the beginning of the late war, and soon after she married a man by the name of Thos. D. Raper, with whom she lived until about the year 1870, when some trouble occurred which compelled Raper to abandon his family apparently forever, at least in a letter to his wife he so expressed himself, stating that it was "pretty hard for a man to have to leave his children forever on account of d--n thieves. It also appears that when this trouble occurred, the Rapers were living in Elko, Nevada, at which time they had three children, the oldest one named Robert, having afterwards died at a place called Sheridan. From 1870 to 1875, we fail to learn anything about her whereabouts during that time. It was in 1872 that the Bender murders were committed, at which time Mrs. Yonkers would have been 28 years of age, she being 41 years old now. That age corresponds with the age of the notorious Kate Bender at that time, but W. A. Graham, who was a deputy sheriff under Major Banney, Sheriff of Cherokee county at that time, says that he knew Kate Bender well, and carried her photograph for four years, and that Mrs. Yonkers is nothing like Kate Bender, either in form or in features, and we think that Mr. Graham is correct, as Kate had very black eyes, while Mrs. Yonkers' eyes are a cold, glittering, gray color.

Among some relics captured in the possession of the prisoner, is a horrible picture or photograph taken both from life and death. The picture represents a coffin…, containing the corpse of a woman, in a standing position, with Mrs. Yonkers dressed in deep mourning, standing on one side and an elegantly dressed gentleman on the other side; what this picture represents is unknown, but it certainly presents a ghastly sight, and makes one shudder to look at it. Our heroine next turned up at South Pueblo in the year 1875 under the name of Susie Stone, which name she assumed until 1882, when she became the wife of Jack Yonkers formerly of Independence County, Ark. In 1879 she was at Alamosa, Colorado. In the year 1881 she ran a stage or hack line from Conejos to San Antonio, Colorado and during that same year she moved to Rio Arriba County, New Mexico, and from thence to Espanola. In June 1882 she bought a Bill of Liquors of Santiago Baca at Albuquerque under the name of Susie Yonkers and took out a saloon license to sell liquors at Wallace where she and her husband, Yonkers, remained until about July 1883, when they loaded up their stock of liquors and went over to Lincoln County. While on the road near Alkali Wells she says Yonkers died with the small-pox and she had to dig him a grave and bury him alone. It was here that she fell in with George Black, who is supposed to have been a witness to the funeral services or the tragedy or whatever it may have been. On arriving at White Oaks, she again assumed the name of Stone, and told that she had lost her

brother at the Alkali Wells with small-pox, but as there was no small-pox in this part of the country at that time, her story was regarded with considerable suspicion and more so when she afterwards said the man was her husband, and again assumed the name of Yonkers. About this time her two sons joined her and they all followed ranching until the following year, when she came to Socorro with Black and they opened up a saloon at the "Walker House. Soon after their arrival here she obtained a bill of sale of Black's team, got him to assign over to her his Lincoln county warrants and every tangible thing of value, and on the 15th day of August, she succeeded in getting Black to deed her his ranch. On the Sunday following, two days after, she shot him twice with a revolver and killed him for which crime she is now in the county jail awaiting trial at the next term of the district court."

DELTA ALTA CALIFORNIA, San Francisco, California, Monday, June 7, 1886:
A Young Woman Who Made Herself the Terror of the Border. Winnemucca Silver State.

Nearly all the old residents of this county will remember Susie Raper. She lived in Paradise Valley in early days, when the Indians were on the warpath, and in one of their raids they killed her brother, Joe Warfield, and in the fight her husband, Thomas Raper, was accidentally shot in the arm and the limb permanently crippled. The family then moved to Dun Glen, where a military post had been established. From Dun Glen they went to Unionville, where Susie made arrangements with a kind-hearted teamster to take herself and children to California. The teamster had five or six yoke of cattle and a regular freighting outfit, and Susie hadn't a dollar, but before they reached California Susie owned the team and the freighter hadn't a cent. She disposed of the team, left her husband, returned to this country, and took up with Captain Robert Payne, of the Nevada volunteers. When Payne's company was mustered out of the service he and Susie went into the cattle and horse stealing business on the Humboldt, near where Carlin is now situated, and, after the organization of Elko County, she was arrested several times for stealing, but, as no jury of twelve men could be impaneled in those days that would find a woman guilty, she was invariably acquitted. Emboldened by her success in escaping through the meshes of the law, Susie continued to increase her herds by appropriating other people's property, and at last, when under arrest by the officers of Elko County she mounted a fleet charger and made her escape, and with Captain Payne left for Colorado Territory. Now she is in jail for the murder of a man with whom she had been living at Socorro, New Mexico. It appears that she prevailed upon the man to deed her his property, and two or three days after he had done so he was killed. Circumstances indicate that Susie had murdered him, and she was charged with the crime and arrested.

## THE IDAHO AVALANCHE, Silver City, Idaho Territory, July 3, 1886:
Susie Raper.

Nearly all the old residents of this county will remember Susie Raper. She lived in Paradise Valley in early days when the Indians were on the warpath, and in one of their raids they killed her brother, Joe Warfield, and in the fight her husband, Thomas Raper, was accidentally shot in the arm and the limb permanently crippled. The family then moved to Dun Glen, where a military post had been established. From Dun Glen they went to Unionville, where Susie made arrangements with a kind-hearted teamster to take herself and children to California. The teamster had five or six yoke of cattle and a regular freighting outfit, and Susie hadn't a dollar, but before they reached California Susie owned the team and the freighter hadn't a cent. She disposed of the team, left her husband, returned to this country, and took up with Captain Robert Payne, of the Nevada volunteers. When Payne's company was mustered out of the service he and Susie went into the cattle and horse stealing business on the Humboldt, near where Carlin is now
situated, and, after the organization of Elko County, she was arrested several times for stealing, but, as no jury of twelve men could be impaneled in those days that would find a woman guilty, she was invariably acquitted. Emboldened by her success in escaping through the meshes of the law, Susie continued to increase her herds by appropriating other people's property, and at last, when under arrest by the officers of Elko County she mounted a fleet charger and made

her escape, and with Captain Payne left for Colorado territory. Now she is in jail for the murder of a man with whom she had been living at Socorro, New Mexico. It appears that she prevailed upon the man to deed her his property, and two or three days after he had done so he was killed. Circumstances indicate that Susie had murdered him, and she was charged with the crime and arrested. - Winnemucca Silver State.

## MESILLA VALLEY DEMOCRAT, Las Cruces, New Mexico, Tuesday, December 14, 1886:
SILVER CITY.

Among the notables at present visiting the city [Silver City] is Mistress Susan Yonkers, more generally known in our locality as "Broncho Sue," however, let it thoroughly be understood that I don't call "Broncho Sue," for they say she is b-a-a-d. Now, there is nothing remarkably strange in Mistress Susan's sojourn in Silver City, because she was sent here from Socorro county by order of the court, and it is a species of nolens volens business with Mistress Susan, but it is strange that her own son, should come down, as I am told he has, to testify against her. He is the same Will Raper (I think it is Will) who was engaged in the La Luz trouble when the lady's last husband was killed, and who was in court at Las Cruces with "the kid," to testify in favor of his mother. Now he has come down to appear against his mother.

## RIO GRANDE REPUBLICAN, Las Cruces, New Mexico, Saturday, December 18, 1886:

Sue Dawson was acquitted of the murder of Robt. Black by a Grant county jury. It was a great legal for her attorney Col. A. J. Fountain.

## MESILLA VALLEY DEMOCRAT, Las Cruces, New Mexico, Tuesday, December 21, 1886:

"Bronco Sue" was acquitted at the recent session of court in Silver City. The testimony of her son, Will Raper, against her was an important factor in her acquittal.

## THE BLACK RANGE, Chloride, Sierra County, New Mexico, Friday, December 24, 1886:

Sue Yonkers, alias, "Bronco Sue," Who has been on trial at Silver City for murder, has been set free.

FORT WAYNE GAZETTE, Fort Wayne, Indiana, Saturday, December 25, 1886:
TOTAL DEPRAVITY.  A LAD WHO TRIES TO HANG HIS MOTHER.
A Specimen of Degradation Without Parallel - The Plans Adopted by a Young Scoundrel to Possess His Mother's Property.
By Telegraph to the GAZETTE.

LAS CRUCES, N.M., Dec. 24 - A very important murder case has just concluded in a verdict of acquittal in the district court at Silver City, the case having been taken there from Socorro on change of venue. In 1883 Robert Black was killed in Socorro, and Susan Yankers [Yonkers], who is also called "Broncho Sue," was arrested for the murder. On her preliminary examination she was discharged, subsequently the grand jury failed to indict her, and she has been living with her two sons on a ranch in Lincoln county for two or three years, where she married Wm. Dawson. In the spring of 1885 Dawson was killed by John H. Good, and while Mrs. Dawson was here attending court prosecuting Good she was arrested and taken to Socorro upon an indictment which had been found but a day or two before the killing of Black. A few days before the trial began in Silver City, this week, it became known that Mrs. Dawson's youngest son, William Raper, was to be a witness against his mother, and it created considerable interest in the case. Young Raper went to the jail to see his mother the day before the trial began and was very affectionate, embracing her, and told her that he knew nothing that would injure her, and he told her counsel the same thing, but after all this he took the stand voluntarily and testified very strongly against his mother. The testimony had shown that Black, at the time he was killed, had thrown a glass at Mrs. Yankers, now Mrs. Dawson, which struck the door jamb, the pieces falling on floor; that Black had then picked up an ax to strike the woman with, and that she then shot him, but the witnesses being separated the son did not hear this testimony, and he swore that his mother told him that she placed the glass and ax there so as to pretend that Black had them and that she might claim that she shot Black in self-defense. He also testified to a conspiracy between his mother, brother, and himself to kill Black, but the facts and circumstances showed his testimony upon this point to be false also. On cross-examination he was compelled to admit that while Good was on trial he (Raper) was also indicted for the part he took in the difficulty which resulted in Dawson's death; that his mother paid $500 to attorneys to defend him; that she mortgaged her property to secure bail for him, and that when he was released he went to Socorro, testified against his mother, and on his testimony mainly the new indictment was found. He admitted having told this story to Dr. Good and others, and that he had never told his mother, and he was forced to admit that he had arrangements made for the disposal of his mother's property after she was hanged or sent to the penitentiary.

While he was testifying, his mother sat with tears running down her cheeks, and afterwards when she was placed on the stand and asked if the statements of her son were true, she hesitated, but finally said that she did not like to help make her son a perjurer. "He is my boy." Her counsel insisted upon an answer, and she did so by saying that the statements were not true. The picture presented by Raper in swearing falsely to hang his mother so that he could get her property so horrified Judge Henderson and all present that the Judge gave great latitude on cross-examination. The counsel, for defense gave Raper a terrible excoriation in their addresses to the jury, and when the jury retired they found a verdict of not guilty as soon as it could be prepared. Mr. Ferguson, district attorney second district, and Attorney-General Dreeder conducted the prosecution; Col. A. J. Fountain and Leonard & Hamilton the defense. The action of young Raper came very near costing him his life, for a party was organized to lynch him, but his mother pleaded for him and he was permitted to escape.

MESILLA VALLEY DEMOCRAT, Las Cruces, New Mexico, Tuesday, January 4, 1887:
VALLEY VARIETIES.
The noted Sue Yonkers came in New Year's very much excited over the loss of a bunch of horses supposed to have been stolen.

MESILLA VALLEY DEMOCRAT, Las Cruces, New Mexico, Friday, January 14, 1887:
VALLEY VARIETIES.

Andy Robertson, the popular deputy sheriff of Lincoln County, came in Tuesday, bringing in Wm. Raper, who is charged with stealing diamonds and Jewelry, worth about $1,000, from his mother, "Bronco Sue." This Will Raper is the same that appeared against his mother at her recent trial in Silver City on the charge of murder. The first official act of Sheriff Ascarate was to receive this noted character and confine him in the county jail.

**MESILLA VALLEY DEMOCRAT, Las Cruces, New Mexico, Friday, March 4, 1887:**

Accounts against the county were examined and approved and ordered warrants to be drawn against the Treasury, to-wit: To Jas. R. Brent, Sheriff Lincoln county, for services and mileage in arrest of Wm. Raper, $101.50.

**MESILLA VALLEY DEMOCRAT, Las Cruces, New Mexico, Friday, March 11, 1887:**

Mrs. Sue Dawson is in the city. Her son Wm. Raper is now in jail on charge of robbing his mother of about $1,000 worth of jewelry.

**MESILLA VALLEY DEMOCRAT, Las Cruces, New Mexico, Friday, July 8, 1887:**
**HORSE STEALING.**

About three weeks ago a number of horses were stolen from Geo. Ganz' ranch. The news did not reach Mr. Ganz, who was in town, till two weeks afterwards. He got onto the track of the bunch and went down to El Paso, Texas, where he made requisition for Jo Raper and Manning, who had taken the stock. Sheriff White lent every assistance in his power and sent a deputy down the Rio Grande. On reaching Fort Rice the deputy heard of his men, but before he could lay hands on them they had heard of him and skipped across the river into Mexico, leaving the animals behind. The officer took charge of the stock and telegraphed Mr. Ganz at El Paso.

Raper and Manning are now under surveillance in Mexico.

Most of the horses taken belonged either to Mrs. Raper or Bill Raper and were held under mortgages, given by both claimants to the stock, to various parties. A few head belonging to other parties were also taken.

**ALBUQUERQUE MORNING DEMOCRAT, Albuquerque, New Mexico, Tuesday, July 12, 1887:**

Joe Raper is accused of stealing stock from his mother, who lives in Las Cruces, and running it over into Mexico. He was aided by a fellow named Manning.

**ALBUQUERQUE MORNING DEMOCRAT, Albuquerque, New Mexico, February 14, 1888:**

Sue Yonkers is the prosecuting witness against Parson Sligh of White Oaks.

## Bronco Sue—Who Was She?

**Based upon research by Charles O. Sanders**

*1914 photo by Charles W. Furlong*

"Bronco Sue" was born Susan Warfield, on September 11, 1844, in New South Wales, Australia. On March 6, 1860, at the age of 15, she married Thomas Davison Raper in Sierra Co., California. About two years later, they moved to Paradise Valley, Nevada where during an 1866 Indian raid, Susan's brother, Joe Warfield, was killed and her husband "accidentally shot in the arm and permanently crippled." They then moved to Dun Glen, where a military camp had been established. From Dun Glen they went to Unionville, then the county seat for Humboldt Co., Nevada. It was in Unionville that Susan's legend began. As the story goes, "Susie made arrangements with a kind-hearted teamster to take herself and her children to California. The teamster had five or six yoke of cattle and a regular freighting outfit, and Susie hadn't a dollar, but before they reached California Susie owned the team and the freighter hadn't a cent." Fact or fiction? It's probably a little of both.

On 22 Jun 1870, Susie was recorded in the United States Federal Census as "S. Raper," a twenty-six year old "Dress Maker," with only her three young sons in her household in the town of Carlin, Elko Co., Nevada. A few months before, in February 1870, Susie had been indicted by an Elko County grand jury on two counts of grand larceny. The first was for the theft of cattle and the second, the theft of jewelry. In March, 1870 she was tried separately on the two counts. Although quickly acquitted on both, newspapers across the nation seized the moment, bestowing upon Susie such monikers as "female buccaneer of the sagebrush," "Lady Gay Spanker of the Pacific" and "Mazeppa of the Humboldt." In May 1870, Susie again captured the attention of the national media with her "Menken ride" through the town of Carlin as she attempted to reclaim her horse Humboldt, taken without her knowledge, by the local constable. On that occasion, it was reported that after having "sprang astride Humboldt" and "threatening the officers with destruction," she "was finally captured, after a liberal exhibition of her well-moulded extremities."

On 23 Mar 1871, Susie's older two sons, "John Raper," age 10, and "Robert Raper," age 8, were admitted (as "half orphans") to the Nevada State Orphan's Home in Carson City, Ormsby Co., Nevada. On 25 Apr 1871, Susie's youngest son, "William Raper," age 5, was also admitted. John Raper was discharged 24 Sep 1872, after which he seems to have changed his first name to Joseph. There is no record of Robert Raper's discharge. Neither does he appear in later records of any type that I can find. So there is a high probability that he died in the orphanage. "William Raper was discharged 12 Feb 1875.

On 25 Jun 1880, Susie, along with her two sons, Joseph Raper, age 19 (formerly known as John), and William Raper, age 14, were recorded in the United States Federal Census as residing in their household in the precinct of the La Jara and Alamosa Valleys in Conejos Co., Colorado. Susie was recorded as "Susan Stone," age 38, a widow, and mother of Joseph, who for whatever reason, was identified as the head of the household. I don't know if there ever existed a Mr. Stone to Susie a widow. That very well could have been nothing more than an alias. I do know that Susie was not a widow by virtue of her first husband, Thomas Davison Raper. He and his crippled limb were in Santa Barbara Co., California before 1880, and he appeared in the "Great Register" of Santa Barbara County through 1896, wherein he was described variously as "Crippled in left arm and hand" and "Left hand crippled."

In 1884 Socorro, New Mexico, Susie would once again attract the attention of newspapers across the country. This time it was as Susan Yonkers for shooting and killing Robert Black in Socorro on or about 17 Aug 1884, a couple of days after he had "deeded his ranch" to her. She was arrested, but released after the grand jury failed to indict.

On 30 Jun 1885, Susie was recorded in the New Mexico Territorial Census as "S. Yonkers," age 42, residing along with her son, William Raper, age 21, in the household of her oldest son, Joseph W. Raper, age 23, in the Penasco Precinct of Lincoln County. Shortly thereafter, Susie married Charles Dawson who was promptly shot and killed by John Hamilton Good on 8 Dec 1885 "about six or eight miles from La Luz." In the murder trial that quickly followed, Susie testified for the prosecution against John Hamilton Good. However, all the publicity surrounding her appearance reminded everyone that she had not been indicted and tried for the killing of Robert Black. That case would be reopened, an indictment secured, and the trial moved to Silver City where it was held in December of 1886. Col. S. M. Ashenfelter, of the Third District, a man of many talents, led the prosecution. He was assisted by the Socorro County District prosecuting attorney, Mr. H. B. Ferguson, and Col. William Breeden, the attorney general of the territory. They were all widely respected brilliant attorneys - the "dream team" of the era. However, even with their star witness, Susie's son William testifying against his mother, they would prove to be no match for Susie and her attorney, Col. Albert J. Fountain. The jury required only two minutes of deliberation before returning a verdict of "Not guilty." The very large crowd present, after cheering their approval, seized Susie's son, William Raper, and attempted to lynch him for "trying to hang his own mother." Susie had not lost her touch.

Susie would garner only limited newspaper coverage over the next two years - and then vanish. The very last sighting of her (I have found) was in the 14 Feb 1888 Albuquerque Morning Democrat. It reads: "Sue Yonkers is the prosecuting witness against Parson Sligh of White Oaks."

Who was "Jack Yonkers," alleged by Susie to have been her husband and portrayed in some 1886 newspapers as having come from Independence Co., Arkansas? I am not at all sure he ever existed. It seems that no one but Susie ever saw him. It's possible he was invented by Susie in order to get the liquor license. If he was real, he may have been Jacob 'Jake' Younckers of Liberty, St Francois Co., Missouri, son of Belshazzar Younckers.

There was much written about Capt. Robert C. Payne, portrayed as Susie's "paramour" and partner in her rustling activities back in Carlin, Nevada. These stories didn't start until 1886, more than fifteen years after they supposedly happened. Capt. Payne did make the news during that era, but it was for leading Company E of the 1st Nevada Cavalry in successful Indian campaigns and the protection of local residents in and around Paradise Valley and Dun Glen. In all the media coverage Susie attracted for her exploits in 1870, there was no mention of Capt. Payne being linked to her in any way. Some modern authors have suggested that Capt. Payne was once an inmate in the Colorado State Penitentiary in Fremont, Colorado. I have found no evidence of that. In the 1880 United States Federal Census, he was recorded residing at the prison, but not in it. There were four people recorded living in the household of the warden. They were the warden, his wife, his daughter and "R. C. Payne," occupation, "Teamster." The only instance I have found where he was recorded as an "inmate" was a month before his death when he was an inmate in the Washington Soldiers Home, Orting, Pierce Co., Washington. The home announced his death on 19 May 1910 writing: "This week we are pained to announce the death of our old comrade in arms, Capt. Robert C. Payne, well known, well liked and well respected in Ferndale and the Northwest." The following week, the Ferndale Record published his obit signed by "Geo. W. Tibbetts, Supt." (of the home). It read: "Gentlemen - Capt. Robert C. Payne died at the Home Hospital May 18th, 1910. He was born in Hudson, New York, June 27th, 1836. He was a single man, engaged in the Livery Business. He enlisted in Company E. 1st Cavalry, April 6, 1864, and was Honorably Discharged November 18th, 1865. He became a member of the Home June 1st, 1909, coming here from Ferndale."

# INTERESTING FACETS OF ABREU FAMILY HISTORY

## By Charles Sanders

*(PastWord Editor's note: Beaubien is pronounced bow BEE an. Abreu is pronounced ah BRA uh. In my youth, I knew some descendents of the Beaubien and Abreu families in Colfax County—which was once a part of the huge Maxwell Land Grant. The Maxwell and Abreu families were intertwined with each other and the history of New Mexico.)*

At one time, rancher and entrepreneur Lucien Bonaparte Maxwell (who lived September 14, 1818 to July 25, 1875) had owned the nation's largest single land holding, once comprised of 1,700,000 acres in New Mexico, and reaching into Colorado.

We all know how Billy "the Kid" Bonney is connected to the Maxwell family: Pete and his sister Paulita Maxwell, children of Lucien B. Maxwell and Luz Beaubien, were Billy's friends. Also, Billy was killed the evening of July 14, 1881 while he was a guest at their home in Fort Sumner.

The fascinating and many-faceted Abreu genealogy is intertwined with the Maxwell and Beaubien family histories, as well as the story of early New Mexico.

Manuel Abreu of Fort Sumner married, at one time, Emilia, and after her death, her sister Odila Maxwell, daughters of Lucien and Luz. Manuel Abreu's sister, Rebecca Abreu, married Juan Cristobal Pablo Beaubien, youngest sibling of Lucien Maxwell's wife, Luz. Manuel Abreu's uncle, Jose de Jesus Gil Abreu, married Maria Petra Beaubien, kid sister of Lucien Maxwell's wife, Luz. Manuel and Rebecca Abreu's mother, and her brother Jose de Jesus Gil Abreu, were among the children of Santiago Abreu, former Mexican governor (1831-1833) of the area that would become New Mexico.

Manuel and Rebecca Abreu's mother was Maria Soledad Abreu, sister of Jose de Jesus Gil Abreu and daughter of Santiago Abreu and María Josefa Refugio Baca. Maria Soledad was first married to Esquipula Caballero on 2 Aug 1839, in Santa Fe, as arranged by and witnessed by then-Governor Manuel Armijo (as well as witnessed by Domingo Fernandes). Much was written on that marriage in George Wilkins Kendall's 1844 *Narrative of the Texan Santa Fe Expedition.*

Maria Soledad next married Dr. John Eugene Leitensdorfer on 6 Dec 1845 in Santa Fe. John Eugene Leitensdorfer was a son of Jean Eugene Leitensdorfer, whose legend is huge and amazing. Soledad's and Dr. John Eugene's marriage was apparently short-lived since we find John Eugene Leitensdorfer back in St. Louis in 1850 living with his widowed mother and his sister, while Soledad is recorded in Santa Fe as Soledad Leitensdorfer living with her widowed mother and Jose de Jesus Gil Abreu. In Manuel Abreu's 1907 sketch/bio, he said his father was Henry Maken, a Frenchman. Soledad's ex-husband, Jean Eugene Leitensdorfer, had remarried in St. Louis on 2 Dec 1850. One record spells his new wife's name as Margaret Michan - another spells it as Margaret Michau. I believe the latter is closer to the correct spelling, which I suspect was Michaud/Micheau, based upon other marriages within the same family. Was Manuel's father, Henry Maken (in the bio), a Michaud/Micheau from the same family into which Soledad's ex-husband had married? Or did Manuel Abreu just confuse the name with that family? In 1860 Santa Fe, we find Soledad had reverted to her maiden name Abreu, and in her household are her two children recorded as "Rebeca Abreu Skinner, age 4, and Manuel Skinner, age 3." Also in her household is Margarita Skinner, age 14, who would marry Cipriano Lara who himself has an interesting bio, published in 1891. Cipriano Lara's recorded achievements included: appointed United States marshal in 1862; a justice of the peace for three terms; and served during the War of 1861-62 as first sergeant of Company A, New Mexico Volunteers.

Following is an interesting passage written in Marlin Aker Jr.'s *The San Luis Valley of Colorado, A short partial History.* "Charles (Carlos) Hippolito Trotier de Beaubien and Antonio Lovato had authority from Governor Don Santiago Abreu of Nuevo Mexico to attempt settlement of the valley by some form of a grant dated February 8, 1833 on behalf of a group of families."

A passage from *Commerce of the Prairies*, by Josiah Gregg: Volume I, Sketches of the History of Santa Fe—at the link: http://www.kancoll.org/books/gregg/gr_ch06_1.htm, described the horrendous torture and murder of Don Santiago Abreu, formerly governor of New Mexico, and "a dozen" others during the New Mexico revolution in 1837.

George Wilkins Kendall told the story of Soledad Abreu in his 1844 "Narrative of the Texan Santa Fe Expedition 3." Link: http://www.tamu.edu/ccbn/dewitt/santakendall3.htm Related links are: http://www.tamu.edu/ccbn/dewitt/dewitt.htm and http://www.tamu.edu/ccbn/dewitt/santafeexped.htm

"The history of this petty, yet most absolute and despotic monarch, Armijo" was included in that story of Soledad, but in not detailed here.

"Don Santiago Abreu, a minister in the administration of Governor Perez and massacred in the former revolution, left a handsome, and, in such advantages as her country afforded, an accomplished daughter, Doña Soledad Abreu. [She was] a maiden whom fifteen summers had ripened into early womanhood. After Armijo's elevation, he insidiously beset the fair doncella with libertine intentions; but she proudly and scornfully resisted all his advances, fortified not more, perhaps, by a sentiment of intrinsic virtue than by the inveterate hatred she entertained for the governor. She knew he had been the mortal enemy of her father, [was] the undoubted instigator of his assassination; such a miscreant could find little favor with the pretty Soledad. But this [powerful] man was not to be so easily foiled, and attempted by intrigue what he had failed to accomplish in a direct way. He influenced a match between Doña Soledad [Abreu] and Esquipulas Caballero, one of his ensigns, and in the plenitude of his good-nature, honored their nuptials by officiating as sponsor at the ceremony.

"He now renewed his vile importunities, and, as he supposed, with better prospect of success. He held, in a manner, the destiny of the young officer in his hands; but in every attempt to accomplish his unholy object, he was most signally baffled. The maiden and the wife proved alike invulnerable to his solicitations and his

threats. At last, convinced of the impregnable virtue of Soledad, he gave up the pursuit, and began making good the deep oaths of vengeance he had often sworn. Her he could not reach directly, but he found means to degrade her unoffending husband and her favorite uncle, who was also a young ensign in his army, named Ramon Baca. Ordering a grand review of the troops, with no other intention than to humble these young cadets, he publicly promoted to a rank above them several officers of inferior grade—a most galling slight in the eyes of a young military aspirant, and a kind of vengeance worthy only of the great Armijo. He even promoted, from the rank of common soldier to a grade above them, a fellow who had been an agent and pander in many of his licentious transactions. The young officers, who were the most deserving and meritorious in the whole corps, now finding themselves at the tail of the army, presented a respectful petition to his excellency, praying to be reinstated. This so irritated the tyrant that he threatened them with instant death if they ever ventured to molest him again with similar importunities, and Caballero, the husband of the pretty Soledad, upon affected suspicion of favoring the disaffected soldiers, was cast into prison with them and heavily ironed!

"Baca, upon some frivolous charge, was ordered out of the country. The 9th of February was the day fixed by the governor for his banishment; but when the time came, the young man declared to his friends that he would not depart, but would raise an insurrection and sacrifice his and their oppressor, or perish in the attempt. With a sword at his side he promenaded the streets of Santa Fé during the forenoon, with great boldness walked directly under Armijo's windows and held conferences with the soldiers. Without a friend to inform him of the young officer's intention, Armijo remained in utter ignorance of the plot; yet the inhabitants were all aware of the intended revolution, and anxiously awaited an outbreak they deemed inevitable. But the good fortune of the despot did not desert him in this extremity. Had a single blow been struck, his power and his oppressions would have ended; for, whenever the star of his destiny tends downward, it will gravitate with a velocity vastly accelerated by the universal hatred in which he is held by his subjects; but when called upon by the heroic Baca, the soldiers at first hesitated ' and then declared that they would render him no assistance. They had promised to aid, to join him; but either from lack of confidence in him as a leader, or from craven fear of Armijo, they were deterred from an open demonstration. Thus was this embryo revolution, which gave such excellent promise, crushed through the timidity of a handful of soldiers.

"In the afternoon, young Baca mounted his horse, and riding to the barracks, made a short speech to his brethren in arms. It was a farewell address, couched in decorous terms, and at its conclusion the really gallant officer departed on his exile. But by this time Armijo had obtained information of the contemplated revolt, and immediately sent off a detachment of dragoons with orders to bring back the young officer, dead or alive. He was overtaken, and thinking himself betrayed by the soldiery, quietly gave up his arms, was guarded back to Santa Fé, and thrust into the same dungeon with his friend, Caballero. At first it was thought that Armijo would order them to immediate execution; but fearing the populace, among whom they had so many friends, he finally sent them off to the city of Mexico to be tried for treason, himself to furnish all the proof. The father of young Caballero, a brave and meritorious officer, but broken down by age and dissipation, was carried to the door of Armijo to intercede for his son; but the tyrant denied him an audience. The shock was too much for the old man: he was borne to his home only to be carried thence to his grave, and his loss was much lamented by both foreigners and natives."

Manuel Abreu married Emilia Maxwell, and his sister Rebecca married Juan Cristobal Pablo Beaubien. Manuel and Rebecca were children of Solidad Abreu, daughter of Santiago Abreu, the former Mexican governor of what would later become New Mexico. I found two old bios, one on J. G. Abreu (Jose de Jesus Gil Abreu) published in 1891, and the other on his nephew Manuel Abreu (married Emelia Maxwell), published in 1907. The bio of Jose de Jesus Gil Abreu (brother of Solidad) ends with the following: "His father, Santiago Abreu, was at one time Governor of New Mexico and held many positions of honor and trust. He was one of the most enterprising citizens in the Territory. He

was killed during the New Mexico revolution in 1837."

The pertinent portion of Manuel Abreu's (son of Solidad Abreu) reads as follows: "His maternal grandfather, Santiago Abreu, was governor of New Mexico under Spanish rule, coming here from old Mexico to enter upon the duties of that position. He was accompanied by his brothers, Marcilino and Ramona Abreu. His father, Henry Maken, was a Frenchman, who came from Canada and married a daughter of Governor Abreu. He died, however, when his son Manuel was but six months old, and the latter afterward took his mother's maiden name."

The part about his father being named "Henry Maken" is somewhat baffling since surname of his sister, Rebecca, was recorded as Skinner in 1860. In this bio they say: "He (referring to Lucien Maxwell) died in 1875 and Pete Maxwell, his son, took charge of the property, but did not keep it up very well...."

The following history of J.G. Abreu comes from *The History of New Mexico: From the Spanish Conquest to the Present Time, 1530-1890: with Portraits and Biographical Sketches of Its Prominent People*, by Helen Haines, published by New Mexico Historical Pub. Co., 1891, original from the New York Public Library, page: 284: "Born in Santa Fe, N. M., September 1, 1823. He received a limited education, but traveled extensively all over the United States, thus acquiring knowledge not otherwise obtained. He was employed by Mr. McCoy, of Kentucky, as a clerk in his business house for four years. Later he went to New Mexico, but returned to Kentucky; here he was left in charge of some mules, but, the party not returning, young Abreu gave them in payment for his debts contracted there. He then went to Independence, Mo., and out of his earnings, fifty cents a day, saved sufficient money to pay for his schooling. In 1848 he removed to Denver, Colorado, and engaged in the mercantile business, being one of the first there. He remained in Denver one year, then returned to New Mexico, settling at Rayado, his present residence. He was married November 26, 1859, to Miss Petra Baubien, the youngest daughter of Don Carlos Baubien, one of the original heirs of the Maxwell Land Grant. They have had twelve children, nine of whom are now living. His father, Santiago Abreu, was at one time Governor of New Mexico and held many positions of honor and trust. He was one of the most enterprising citizens in the Territory. He was killed during the New Mexico revolution in 1837."

And in *History of New Mexico: Its Resources and People*, by George B. Anderson, published by Pacific States Pub. Co., 1907, page 887:

"Manuel Abreu is one of the New Mexico's native sons and a representative of one of the old, distinguished and prominent families of the Territory. His maternal grandfather, Santiago Abreu, was governor of New Mexico under Spanish rule, coming here from old Mexico to enter upon the duties of that position. He was accompanied by his brothers, Marcilino and Ramona Abreu. His father, Henry Maken, was a Frenchman, who came from Canada and married a daughter of Governor Abreu. He died, however, when his son Manuel was but six months old, and the latter afterward took his mother's maiden name.

"Manuel Abreu was born in Santa Fe, New Mexico, in June, 1857, and in 1873 went to Fort Sumner, where he engaged in the sheep business in connection with his brother-in-law, Pablo Beaubien, a son of Charles Beaubien, who was the original owner of the Maxwell land grant. Carlos Beaubien and Miranda were the original grantees from the Spanish government. Lucien Maxwell, a French-Scotchman, born June 24, 1829, married Luz Beaubien, a daughter of Carlos Beaubien, and Mr. Maxwell later bought the largest part of the grant from Mr. Beaubien, and after his death purchased the remainder from the heirs. About 1870 Mr. Maxwell sold the grant to a company for six hundred thousand dollars, at which time he removed to old Fort Sumner on the Pecos River, then located in San Miguel County. He purchased the improvements [but not the land they sat on] at the fort from the government and turned his attention to cattle and sheep raising, and farming. He began to further improve the property, taking ditches from the Pecos River, and soon developed a beautiful place. He died in 1875 and Pete Maxwell, his son, took charge of the property, but did not keep it up very well, and about 1885 sold out to the Fort Sumner Land & Cattle Company, while he and others moved down the river, one mile, and

started the town of Fort Sumner, which is in existence today. There Pete Maxwell, who was born April 27, 1848, lived until his death on the 21st of June, 1898. Manuel Abreu began sheep raising in 1873, and has continued therein to the present time. He also conducts a store in Fort Sumner in connection with his sheep and stock business. He is a representative of one of the prominent old Spanish families of the Territory and is displaying modern business enterprise in the conduct of his interests here."

## History of Dedrick Tintype of Billy the Kid That Sold for $2.3 Million in 2011

### By Jan Girand

Legend says there had been four tintype photos taken of Billy Bonney by an itinerant traveling photographer with a ferrotype box camera in the winter of 1879-1880 outside Beaver Smith's saloon in old Fort Sumner. According to Paulita Maxwell, the photographer was just taking down his equipment when Billy arrived and asked to have his photo taken. The four identical images, each just two inches by three inches on one metal plate, cost Billy 25¢. Years later,

Dan Dedrick, a pal of Billy's, told his nephew Frank Upham that the photographer had just taken a photo of him shortly before he took Billy's. He had been present when Billy's famous photo was taken.

Walter Noble Burns wrote in 1925 that the chain of custody of the Billy tintype, according to Paulita, was: From Billy to Maxwell house servant Deluvina, to Paulita's mother, Luz, to Paulita's sister, Odila, and it was passed on to John Legg, and finally to Charlie Foor.

Following is an excerpt from Burn's 1925 *The Saga of Billy the Kid* (pages 194 – 196):

The only photograph Billy the Kid ever had taken was in possession of the Maxwell family for many years.

"It was taken by a traveling photographer who came through Fort Sumner in 1880," says Mrs. Jaramillo. "Billy posed for it standing in the street near old Beaver Smith's saloon. I never liked the picture. I don't think it does Billy justice. It makes him look rough and uncouth. The expression on his face was really boyish and very pleasant. He may have worn such clothes as appear in the picture out on the range, but in Fort Sumner he was careful of his personal appearance and dressed neatly and in good taste.

"We had an old servant living with us who went by the name of Deluvina Maxwell. My father had bought her as a child for fifty dollars from a wandering band of Navajo Indians and she had been in our family ever since. Billy the Kid was Deluvina's idol; she worshipped him; to her mind, there never was such a wonderful boy in all the world. When Billy was locked up in the Fort Sumner calaboose after his capture at Arroyo Tivan, Deluvina went to visit him. It was a cold winter's day and, as the little jail was unheated, Deluvina came home and got a heavy scarf she had knitted and took it to her hero. In return for this kindness, the Kid gave her his only photograph, which he had carried around in his pocket. He would have given Deluvina nothing she would have prized more.

"My mother kept the picture in a cedar chest for years, and finally my sister, Odila, gave it to John Legg, a Forth Sumner saloon keeper and friend of the family. Legg was shot and killed and Charlie Foor, an executor of his estate, came into possession of the picture. When Foor's house was burned down, the original was destroyed but fortunately many copies of it had been made. A wash drawing made from this photograph hangs in the Governor's Palace at Santa Fé."

Foor, who acquired one of those tintypes, had arrived in Fort Sumner just months after Billy was killed. After his fire, it was generally believed proof of the only likeness of Billy was lost forever.

According to a 1999 published report by John W. and Robert E. McNellis of El Paso Texas, Jarvis Garrett—while going through his sister, Elizabeth's, belongings in Roswell after her death—had found a trunk or box filled with items of historical value. Jarvis said it included tintypes (perhaps plural) of Billy, like the one later in possession of the Lincoln County Heritage Trust. Jarvis said an author, researching and writing a book about Billy, had borrowed from his mother—Apolinaria Garrett, wife of Patrick Garrett—a tintype of Billy, and possibly other historical treasures, which he never returned. Because of that writer, said Jarvis, Mrs. Garrett became bitter. She lost faith and any trust of the inquiring public, decreeing that nothing more of Patrick Garrett's memorabilia was to be accessible to outsiders.

In 1985 the public became aware of the Dedrick-Upham tintype. That tintype had been given away by Billy and ultimately passed to his pal, Dan Dedrick, who died in 1938.

In the eighteen-hundreds, Dan's brother, Sam, was co-owner of a livery stable in White Oaks, New Mexico, where Billy the Kid often stopped over. From that livery, Sam Dedrick sold horses that Billy had stolen. Years later, that Sam Dedrick family owned a ranch in Mexico, near Chihuahua. Sam, one-armed because of an old injury, had been an American rancher and miner in that area of Mexico for at least sixteen years. According to newspaper accounts, he died March 5, 1909, shortly after being fatally shot by Panofilo Torrez, a ranch hand, in Chihuahua, Mexico.

The provenance through the years of the tintype that had belonged to Dan Dedrick is indisputable. It had passed down to his nephew Frank Upham, the family of Marcheta Upham and Elizabeth Upham. Just three years earlier, in May, 1999, Elizabeth wrote a letter, published in an Outlaw Gazette issue, reporting on the tintype.

She said she had spent considerable time talking to author Gale Cooper, providing her with information about the tintype for a book she was researching and writing. Elizabeth referred her to Marcheta for more information. They later never again heard from Cooper. Marcheta died August 19, 1999. Elizabeth said Cooper had taken a photograph of the tintype while it was still with the Lincoln County Heritage Trust in Lincoln. Elizabeth said the resulting image she saw was poor, darkened. She said the earlier images taken of that tintype she had seen were much better quality. Did the condition of the tintype deteriorate?

The Upham family had loaned the tintype to the Lincoln County Heritage Trust, and it was in their possession from 1986 to 1998, until the Trust disbanded. Then the tintype was returned to its owner, Frank Upham. During some of those years, it was displayed in the LCHT museum in Lincoln. During that time, the Trust had conducted studies of the tintype by historians and forensic experts. Photographic experts from Eastman Kodak also came and offered to take the tintype to their labs, where they had the latest and best photographic technology, to restore and preserve it, but it was said that the Trust declined that offer.

In 1989, the LCHT commissioned renowned forensic anthropologist Clyde Snow to do a computer study of the tintype. One of his projects was to compare the image on the tintype—the one and only known still-existing and indisputable image of Billy—to images of "Brushy Bill" Roberts as well as other photos claimed by some to also be of Billy. Using 25 facial "landmarks"—facial features that never change—the computer analysis disproved, beyond a doubt, Brushy Bill's claim to be Billy Bonney. It also proved, beyond much doubt, that the other 150 photos compared to Billy's tintype were not The Kid.

Except for the years it was loaned to the LCHT, almost from its beginning, the tintype was always in the possession of the Dedrick-Upham family, who had kept it locked away in a safe, for posterity. Members of the Upham family who saw the tintype, before and after it had been loaned to the LCHT, claimed it had become damaged, almost totally blackened. Some of those involved with the Lincoln County Heritage Trust, then serving on the board, or called to Lincoln to work on the project, also claimed the tintype had been damaged while it was there. If that is true, why was that not publicized? And if so, was it later restored?

The tintype, after considerable international publicity, was auctioned in June 2011 in Denver, Colorado by Brian Lebel at his annual Old West Show and Auction. Frank Upham's collection auctioned that day also included a tintype of his uncle Dan Dedrick, taken just before Billy's world-famous photo was "snapped" by the same photographer. The price the BTK tintype bought, $2.3 million, purchased by a Florida collector of western history memorabilia, broke all records for sale of a photograph.

Is the history of that tintype yet another enduring Billy mystery that has no answers?

## Provenance of the Dedrick-Upham BTK Tintype
### Research by Charles O. Sanders

Prior to sale at auction, the final owner of the tintype was Frank Upham. It had passed to Frank through his mother, Malinda Dedrick Upham. Following is the family genealogy:

The tintype passed from Daniel Charles Dedrick (who died 25 April 1938) to Frank Lester Upham. On 18 April 1930 census, those two households—Daniel Charles Dedrick and Frank Lester Upham—were recorded as two doors from one another in Hayfork, Trinity, California. Frank was the son of David Upham and Malinda Dedrick. Malinda was the sister of Daniel Charles, Sam and Mose Dedrick. Their parents were Jacob P. Dietrich and Leah Greenawalt.\

Frank Lester Upham's wife was Sarah Elizabeth Transure, whose first husband had been Frank's brother, Harry K. Upham. Frank Lester Upham and Sarah Elizabeth Transue were the parents of Frank T. Upham; he married Marian Elizabeth Sturtevant. Frank and Marian Elizabeth Upham were the final owners of the tintype before its sale at auction.

Photos on this page are from the Library of Congress; they placed no restrictions on publishing these images. By research, they were brought to you by Charles O. Sanders.

New Mexico became the 47<sup>th</sup> state of the U.S.A. on January 6, 1912 when U.S. President William Howard Taft signed the Proclamation in Washington DC, following the Act of Congress that passed in 1910.

It is this day, January 6, 1912, 100 years ago, that New Mexico is celebrating all year in 2012 with multiple events throughout the state, for this once in a lifetime anniversary.

## Charles O. "Butch" Sanders

### By Jan Girand

Charles O. Sanders, better known as Butch, lives near Dover, Delaware with his wife, Barb. Butch was born in northern Kentucky in 1943. He attended the University of Kentucky; upon graduation in May 1967 he was commissioned into the Air Force. He completed Undergraduate Pilot Training (UPT) at Moody AFB, Georgia and T-38 Pilot Instructor Training (PIT) at Tyndall AFB, Florida.

His first assignment out of PIT was Laredo AFB, Texas as a T-38 Instructor Pilot. After three years in Laredo, Butch's long awaited assignment to Vietnam came down. But it wasn't exactly the fighter for which he had volunteered. It was an AC-119 gunship - aka the "Flying Coffin." In October 1972, he completed the AC-119G phase of that training near Columbus, Ohio just as a secret peace agreement was signed with North Vietnam. Butch's assignment was cancelled and he was reassigned (or "exiled" as he calls it) as the commander of an Air Force detachment on an Army Post in New Jersey (Fort Monmouth).

After two years in exile, he was rescued and sent to Dover AFB, Delaware where he flew the C-5 Galaxy for the next 24 years until his retirement in October 1998. He logged around 8,000 hours in the C-5 and was a squadron Chief Pilot and the Chief of Wing Standardization/ Evaluation. Butch flew the C-5 in airlift support of military operations around the world from 1974 through the 1st Gulf War. Most required 24-hour crew duty days; missions served well by the C-5's two bunkrooms, two kitchens and two real flush toilets. He says it doesn't get any better than that.

During his early Air Force years, Butch's passion was Mayan archaeology and photography. He combined the two, spending his annual 30-days of leave every year traveling around the land of the Maya (Mexico, Belize, Guatemala and Honduras) taking photographs—and the other 11 months of each of those years developing, processing and printing them.

Butch says he became involved with genealogy, like most of us, searching for his own family history. He then began researching old west notables like Calamity Jane, Wild Bill Hickok, Buffalo Bill, Annie Oakley, Wyatt Earp, Jesse James, Billy the Kid and scores of others. That included the likes of Elmer McCurdy, the last old west outlaw to be buried; shot and killed in 1911, but not buried until 1977 when he was found "hanging" on the set of the "Six Million Dollar Man." Butch has also done extensive research on imposters J. Frank Dalton and Brushy Bill (who started his show business career as a bit player in the J. Frank Dalton traveling sideshow). Among other imposters he has researched are Henry Street Smith and John Miller. He notes that Henry Street Smith is found in the 1900 census living in the Lincoln County household of George W. Coe, which explains his knowledge of Billy. In Butch's opinion, John Miller has been much maligned as a Billy the Kid claimant since he never made that claim. His biographer and adopted son made it for him.

Butch's approach is a little different than most. He researches not only his subject, but his subject's family history, their neighbors, the biographers and the sources the biographers used.

*John Halvorson Photo*

Jan Girand lives with her husband, Dan, in Roswell, New Mexico. Countless generations of her mother's family have lived, in continuity, in northern New Mexico. Two lines—both parents of her great-great-grandmother—have been traced back to Onate's 1595 expedition into New Mexico.

Jan was a newspaper reporter; was published in the New Mexico Magazine; wrote and published a non-fiction book and produced five annual issues of a history magazine. Jan owns and publishes a long-term Internet magazine www.roswellwebmagazine.com, and is owner and editor of an independent publishing company, YellowJacketPress, which has published several books.

Jan is especially interested in regional New Mexico history. She is the producer and editor of *PastWord*, an annual publication, with multiple contributors, that covers characters and events of New Mexico's turbulent 1800s. She is also currently researching, compiling and writing, along with multiple contributors, several family history books that include considerable regional New Mexico history, mostly of the 1800s. Those books will include copies of early documents and actual vintage transcripts of court cases.

Visit her websites: www.yellowjacketpress.com and www.past-word.com

Jan can be reached at: editor.pastword@gmail.com and yellowjacket@cableone.net

Back cover design by Kathy Avery incorporates photo taken by Ed Cook of Patrick Garrett statue. "Ride to Destiny" is a majestic bronze statue by Texas sculptor Robert Summers, dedicated March 31, 2012. It is located on Virginia Street, Roswell New Mexico facing the (new) main entrance to the 1912 Chaves County Courthouse. This huge statue of the 6-foot 5-inch tall Patrick Floyd Jarvis Garrett, 1850-1908, on horseback, loading his favorite 44-40 colt hand-gun, visualizes him in July 1881 as he begins his 80-mile ride to Fort Sumner in search of the illusive Billy the Kid Bonney.

www.ingramcontent.com/pod-product-compliance
Lightning Source LLC
Chambersburg PA
CBHW052341100426
42736CB00046B/3344

*9780615661117*